Zen Doodle Drawing:

Unleash You Imagination with Amazing
Zen Doodle Drawing

By Elizabeth Stone

Table of Contents

Introduction

Chapter 1 – What is Zen Doodling?

Chapter 2 – How to Draw a Zen Doodle?

Chapter 3 – Zen Art Meditation

Chapter 4 – Subconscious Drawing

Chapter 5 – Zen Doodle Coloring Books for Adults

Chapter 6 – Crafts Similar to Zen Doodling

Conclusion

Disclaimer

While all attempts have been made to verify the information provided in this book, the author does assume any responsibility for errors, omissions, or contrary interpretations of the subject matter contained within. The information provided in this book is for educational and entertainment purposes only. The reader is responsible for his or her own actions and the author does not accept any responsibilities for any liabilities or damages, real or perceived, resulting from the use of this information.

The trademarks that are used are without any consent, and the publication of the trademark is without permission or backing by the trademark owner. All trademarks and brands within this book are for clarifying purposes only and are the owned by the owners themselves, not affiliated with this document.

Introduction

Having a hobby is an awesome thing. It allows you to do something productive with your spare time, instead of just lying down and watching TV the whole day. Still, a hobby can become much more than just a tool for fighting boredom, but for that, you need to choose the right kind of hobby.

If you're looking to open up your mind to new things and allow it to be creative, at least for a couple of hours every day, then perhaps Zen Doodle drawing is the right kind of craft for you. This art is proven to be a great way to boost your creativity and can spark new ideas easily. These ideas are not only related to art, which is actually why this craft is growing so popular around the world. Zen Doodle drawing can be the beginning of a new part of your life, the creative part.

Once you let the artist within you free, they'll be able to produce ideas you couldn't even imagine. You will be able to think of the best solution to your business and love life, and perhaps even create something huge. But, there's no need to go far, if Zen Doodle drawing just helps you to relax and forget about the problem, then we can say that its job is done.

We hope that we've managed to interest you in Zen Doodle drawing. We promise that if you continue reading the book, you will have a good time. Here, you'll find everything you should know about this craft, from its history to how to do a drawing.

Chapter 1 – What is Zen Doodling?

Zen Doodling is an art technique of drawing a simple thing or an abstract object, following a few rules. The most important feature of this type of art is that the drawing moves need to be repeating. Apart from being an interesting craft, Zen Doodling is a great way of meditation for many people.

Without any doubt, Zen Doodling belongs to the category of affordable crafts. In fact, this is one of the cheapest arts to perform, needing only a few things to begin with – a piece of paper, a pen. Still, the whole point of Zen Doodling isn't material things, but spiritual. To become great in this art, you need a bit of spare time and a lot of will. As you progress, you will find that there are other objects you can use in order to make your drawings more interesting, such as rulers, for example.

One of the best things about Zen Doodling is that you don't have to have a goal every time. You can simply set your mind free and let it take you and the drawing wherever. You start with one line and go one step at a time, not planning the final look of the drawing. That allows you to stop drawing any time you feel like it and continue again, when the inspiration strikes.

Perhaps the best thing about Zen Doodle drawing is that can use them for all sorts of things. You can use this print for pillows, purses, clocks, coffee mugs, etc. Actually, you can decorate anything that comes to your mind, which includes even pieces of clothes and shoes. Actually the sky is the limit, literary. Once you craft the Zen Doodle drawing, you can apply it everywhere. In that case, you will not need patterns. You will be able to draw directly on the surface such as, let's say for an example, an office or kitchen wall.

Chapter 2 – How to Draw a Zen Doodle?

First of all, you will need a piece of blank paper. The best would be a square, but any shape is good. Now take a pen and draw the first object. It's up to you what that object would be. It can be an abstract shape, but it can be some something else. Do not think too much about it; just let your hand do the work! Once you've done with the first object, you need to leave it as it is, without making any corrections.

Within the drawn shapes freely draw the new lines, as if you want to share the object by several smaller pieces. Also, do not press lines. When you are finished with it, you can fill every part of a particular pattern. Tracery may consist of triangles, squares, circles, dots and all other forms. Use a pen or a marker to bold the patterns in order to create shadows and gave additional depth to the drawing.

What matters about Zen Doodle drawing is that the eraser is never used. That sends the message that there is no possibility of turning back and correcting errors. There is only here and now and the only thing you do is draw some patterns with the ubiquitous care and concentration. Zen Doodle drawing rule requires drawing with a black pencil or ink on white paper, but you can add color if you want.

Surely the best way to demonstrate Zen Doodle drawing is with an example. Practice beats theory in this case, so here are six different examples with how-to-do guidelines.

How to Draw a Puppy?

You start drawing a puppy with two simple circles, which should be the puppy's eyes. Also do a simple contour of its head and body.

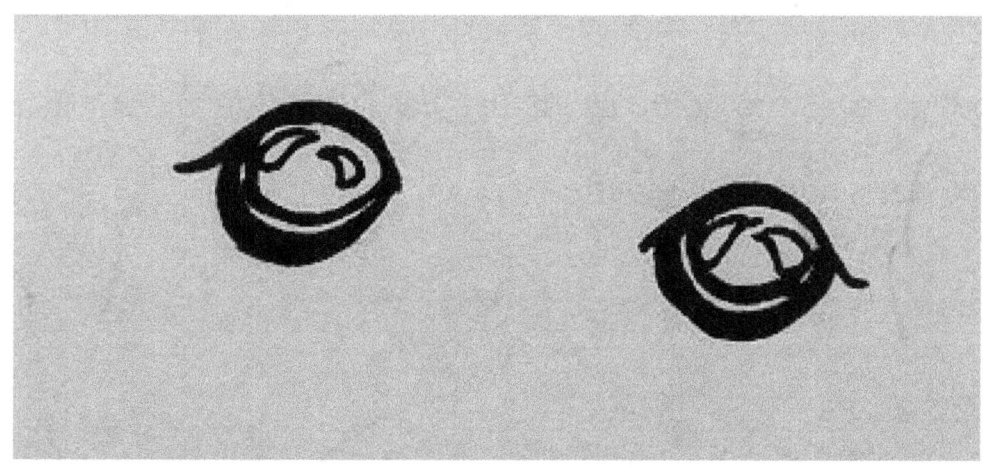

The next step is to finish with the eyes by adding the pupil and eyelashes. Also, draw a few other face features, like nose and eyebrows.

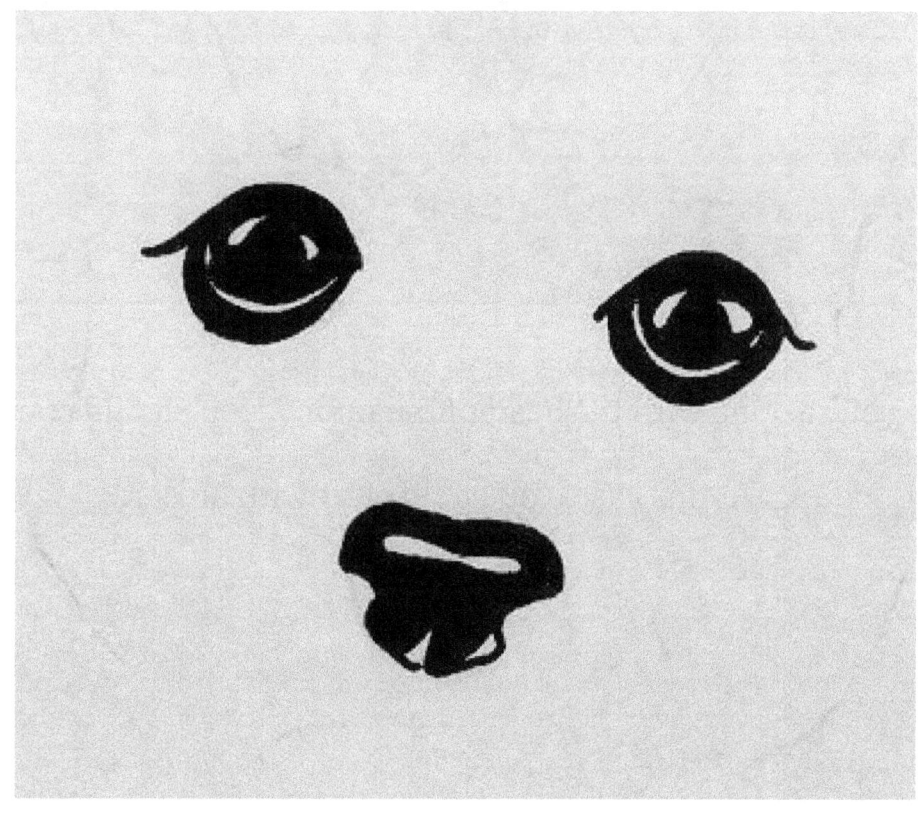

Now go over the contours of the head, bolding the lines that make ears, nose, and mouth.

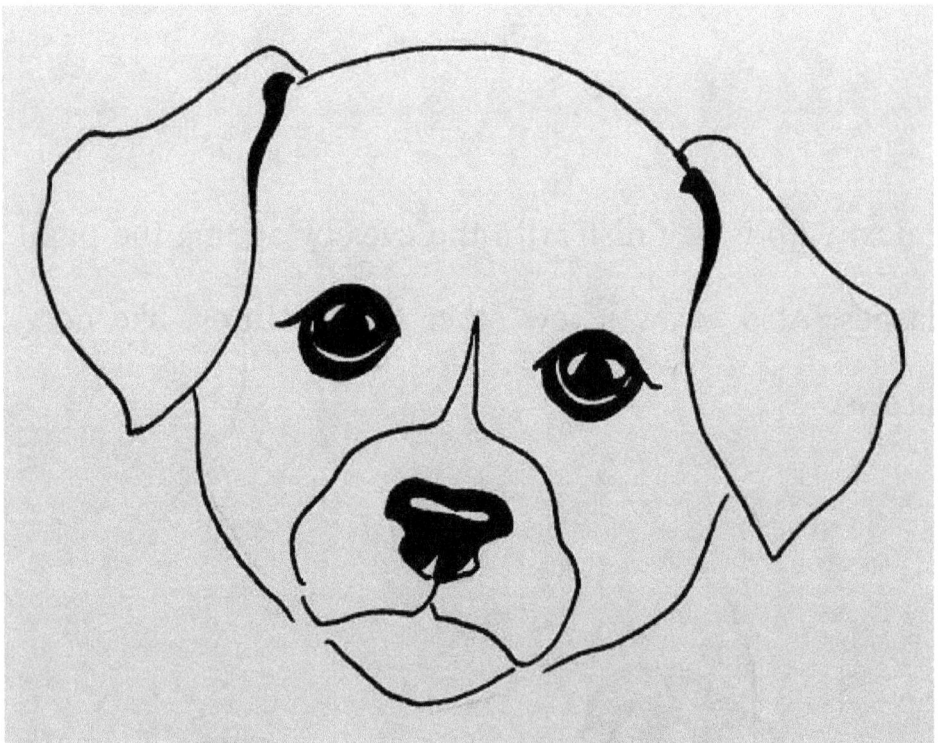

Once you're done with the head of the puppy, you should start Zen Doodling. In this case, you could start with an ear.

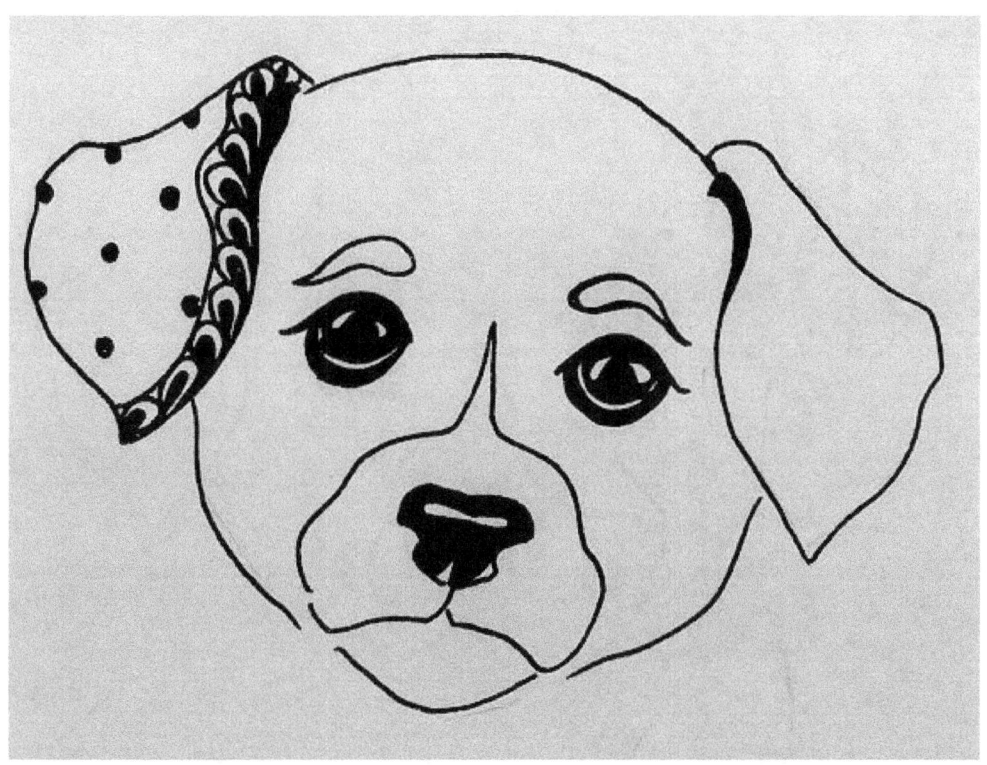

Let your mind go and fill the whole area of ear with doodles. In the example, you can see how a spider web doodle looks like.

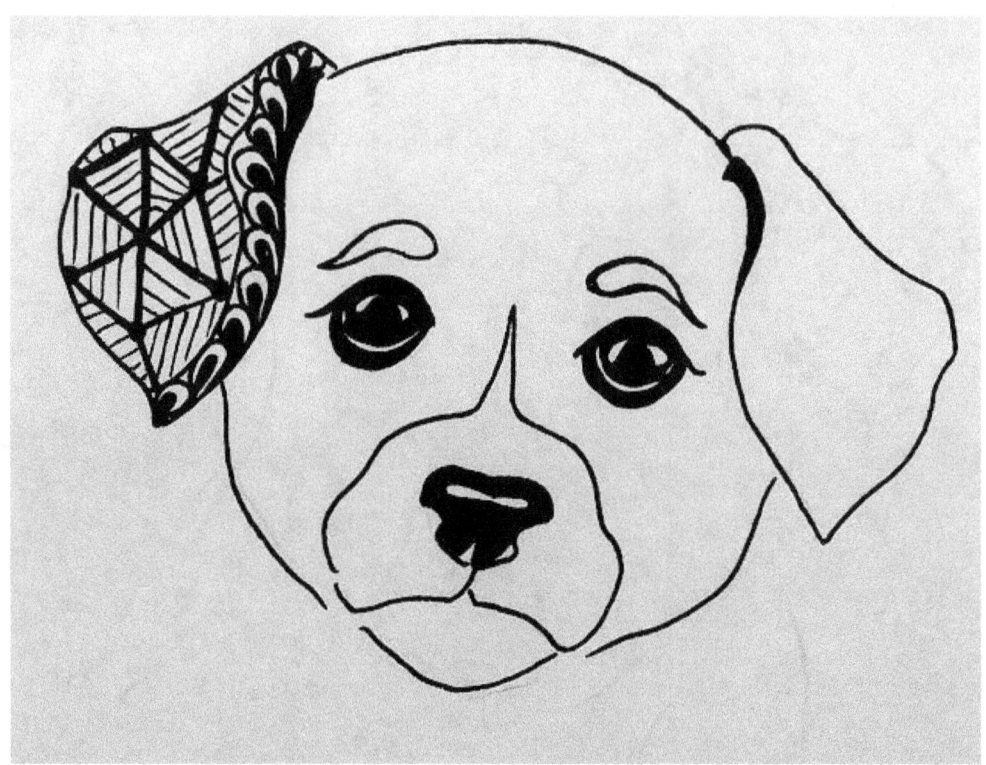

Do the same with the face, being careful not to interfere with other parts. You can do some flowery ornaments, like you can see here.

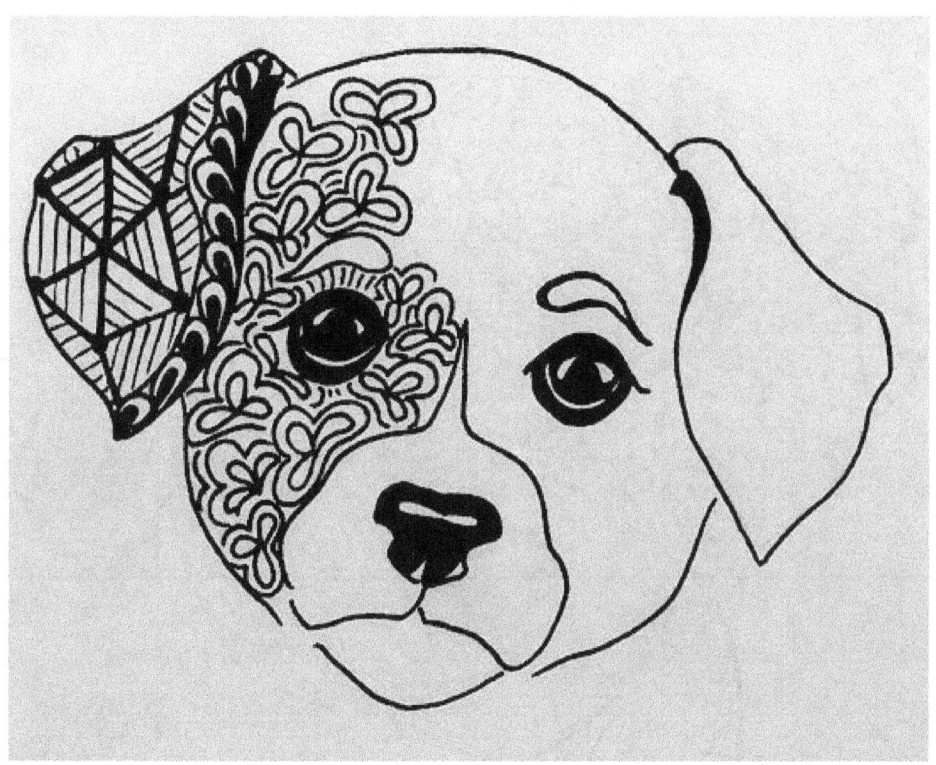

Cover the whole head with doodles, but be careful to do different doodles on each part of the head. For example, you can fill the other ear area with triangles.

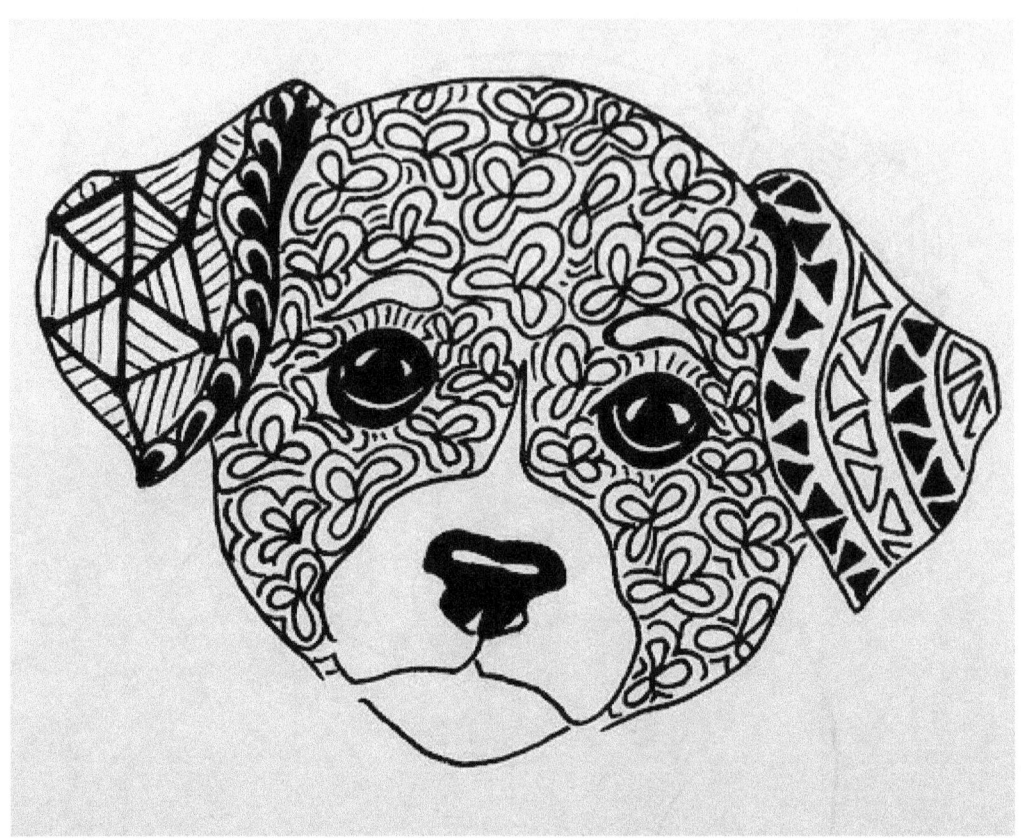

When you're done with the puppy's head, do the same with its body.

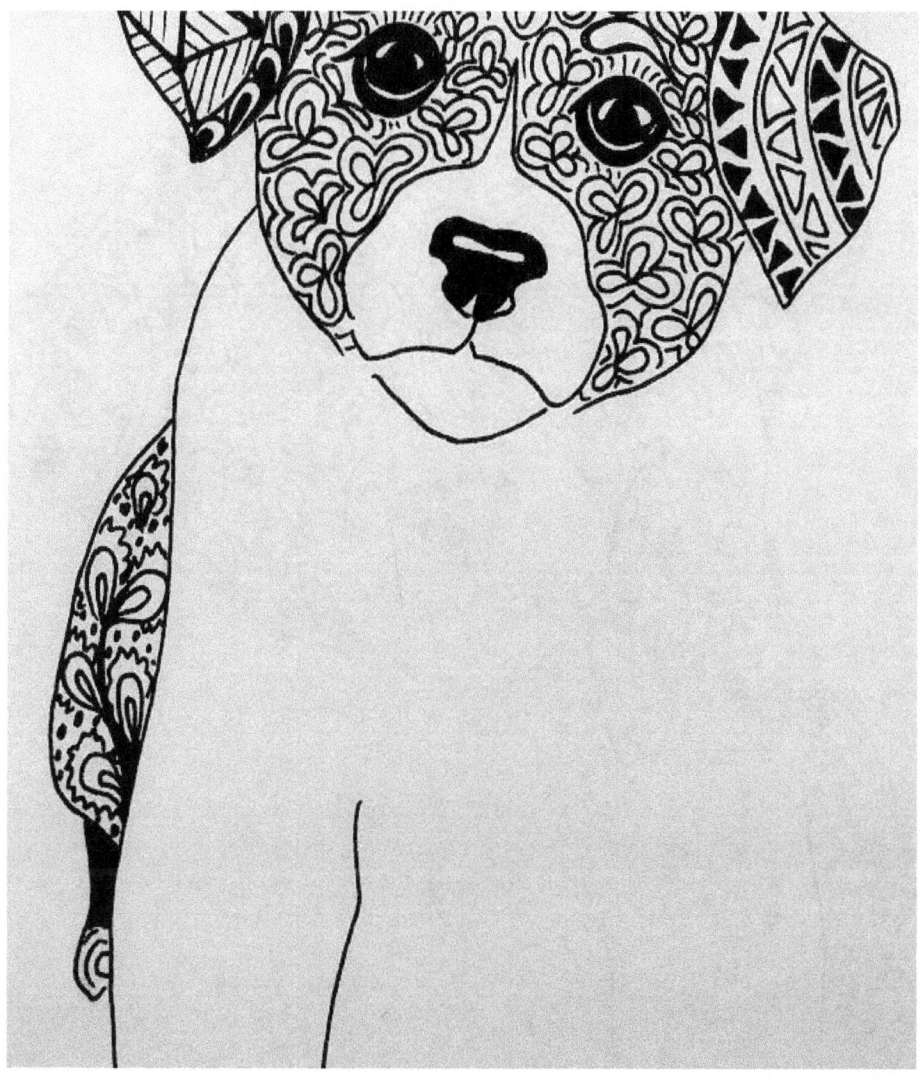

While adding doodles, be careful to add different ones on different parts of the body.

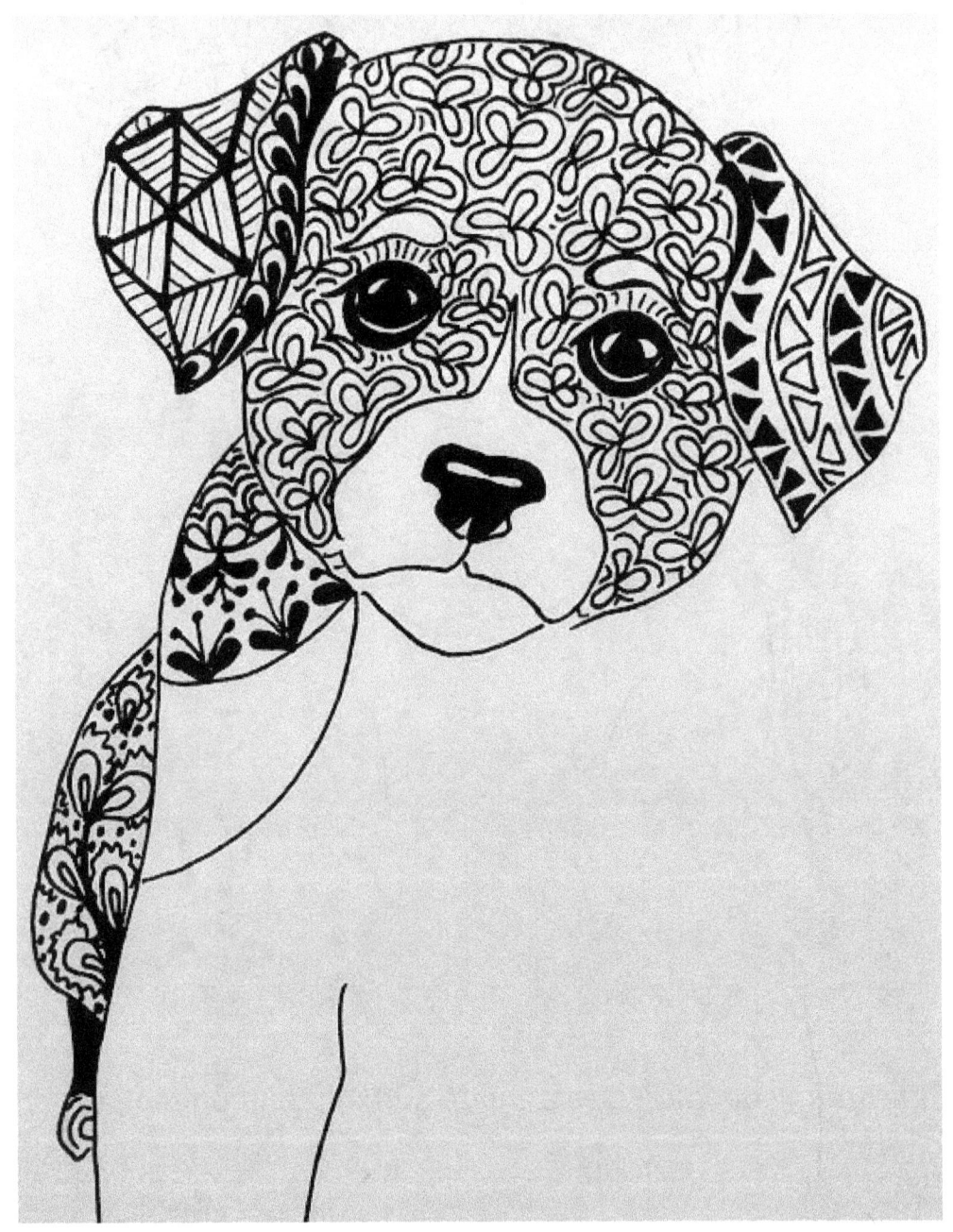

Draw different style of doodles on its front leg, back leg, shoulder, etc. As you can see in the example, you can use all sorts of shapes, from snowflakes to flowers.

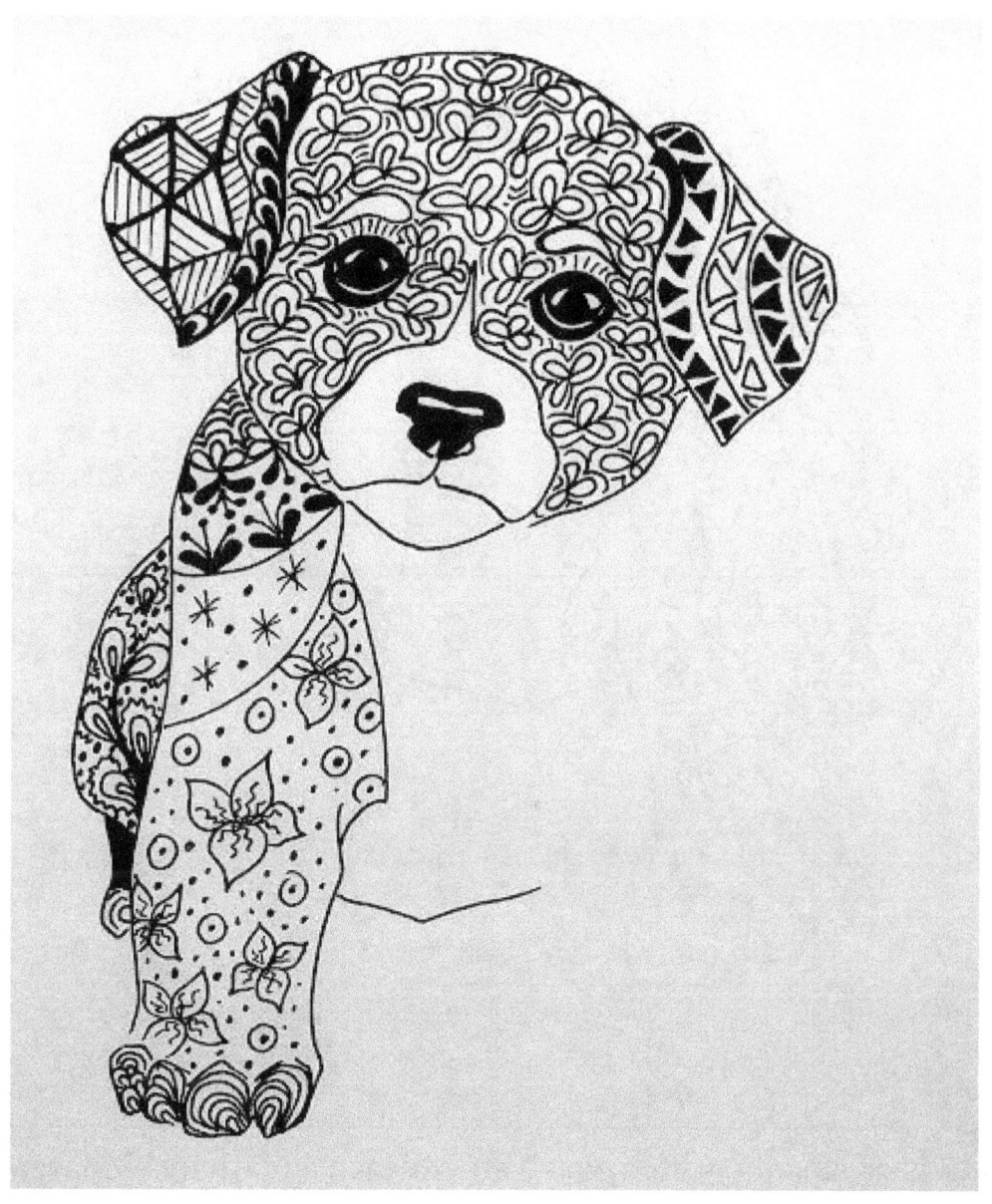

The more different styles of Zen Doodles you use, the final work will be more interesting. Here, you can see flowers of puppy's front leg, flakes on one shoulder and spiral lines on the other.

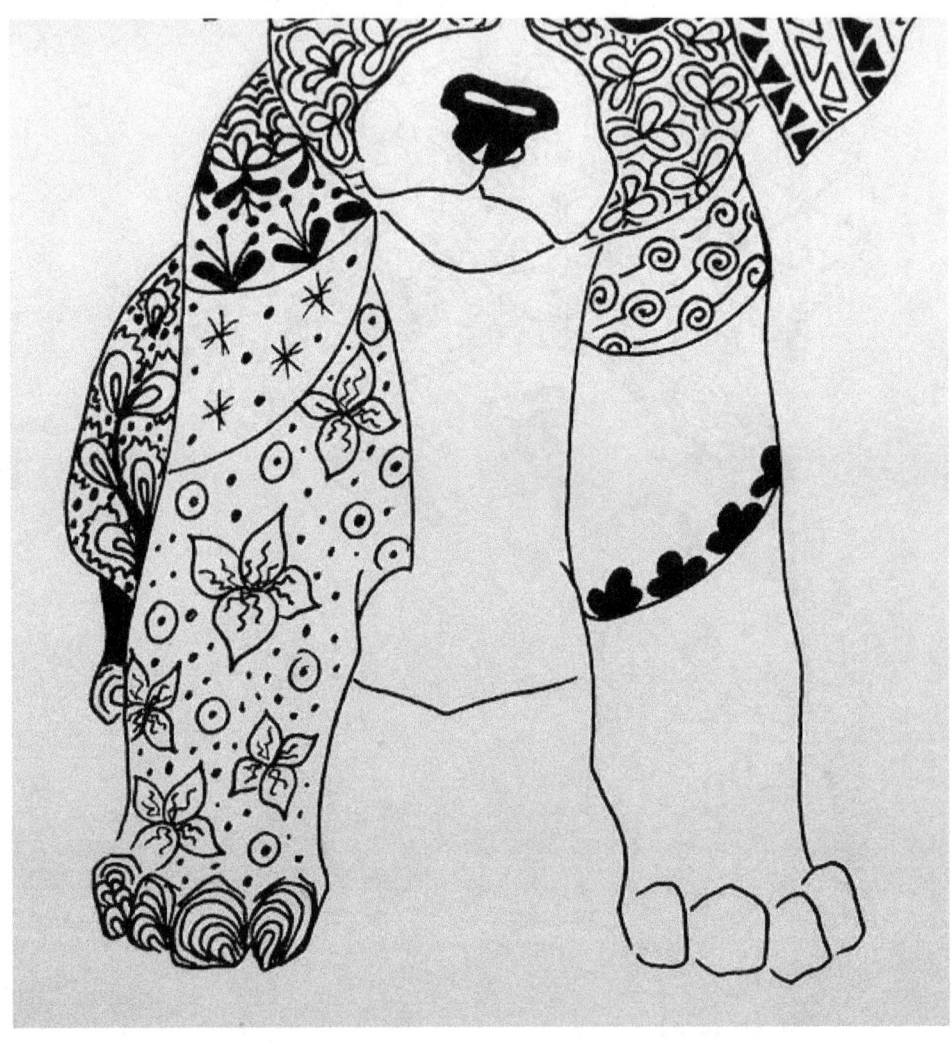

This is a step in which you can unleash creativity – it really doesn't matter how many different doodles you do, or their styles. Do those as you please.

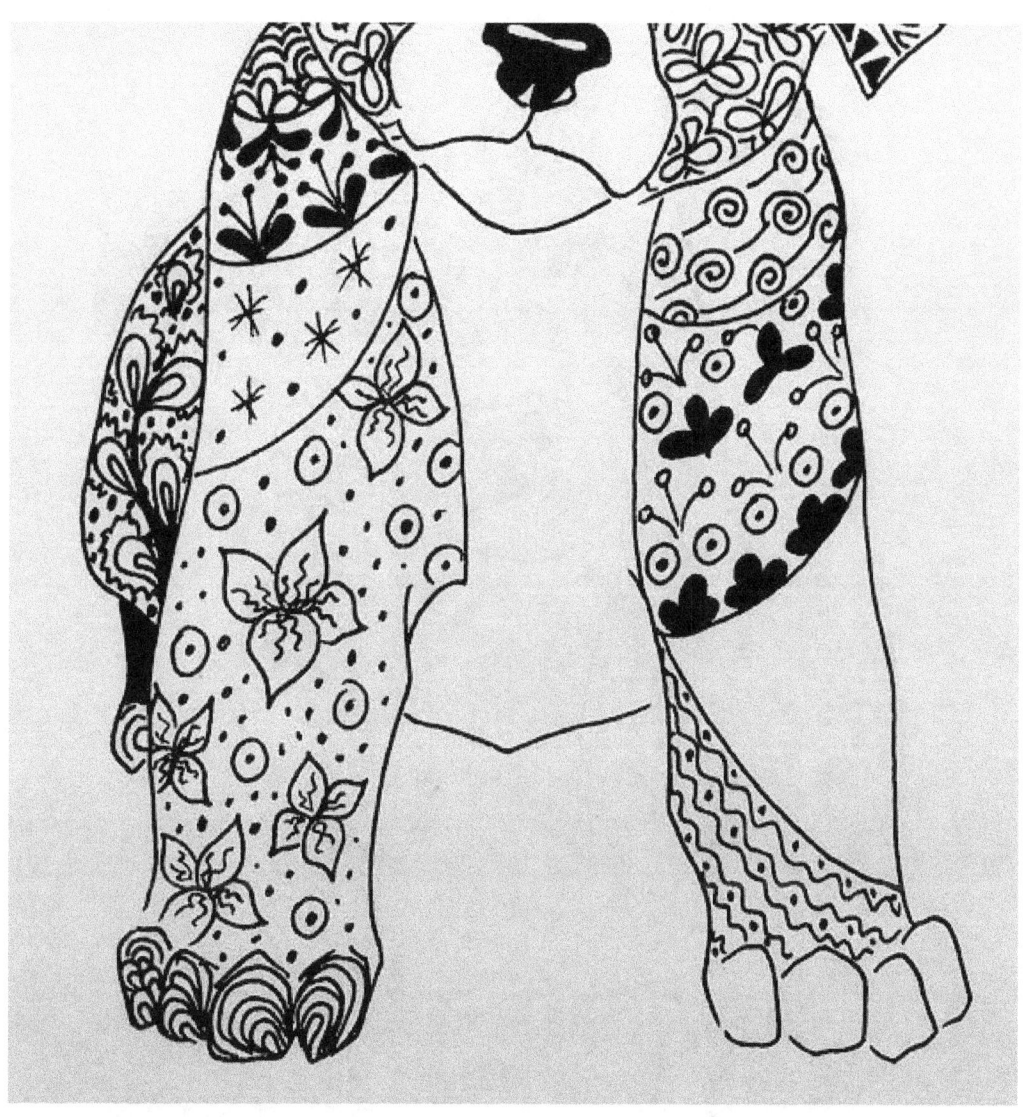

If you wish, you can leave the tummy of the puppy blank for the

final touch.

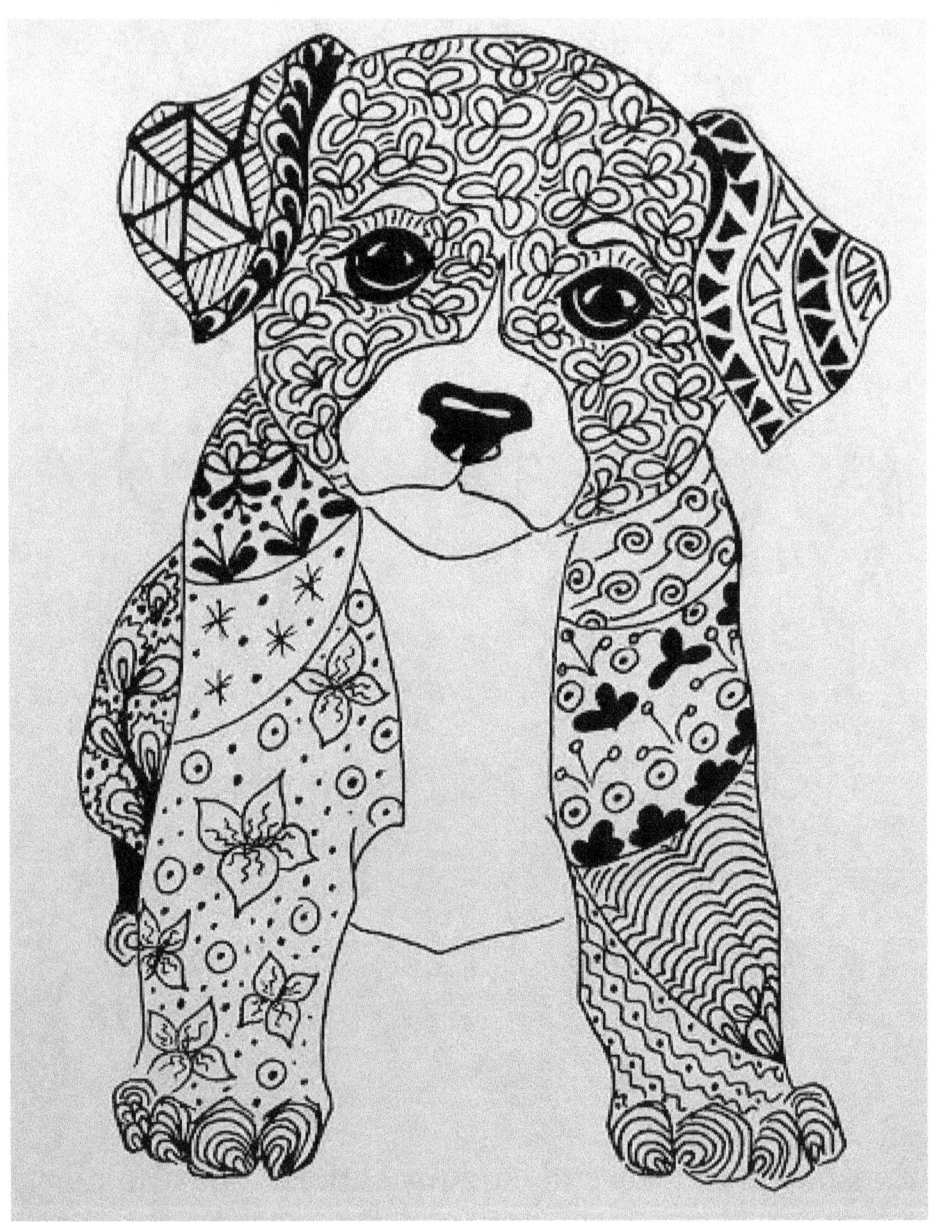

At this point, there should be several different types of doodles on the puppy's body - three or four of them on each leg, ears and head.

The final picture shows how the drawing should look like, but whatever you draw it will be beautiful as it'll be a sign of your personality.

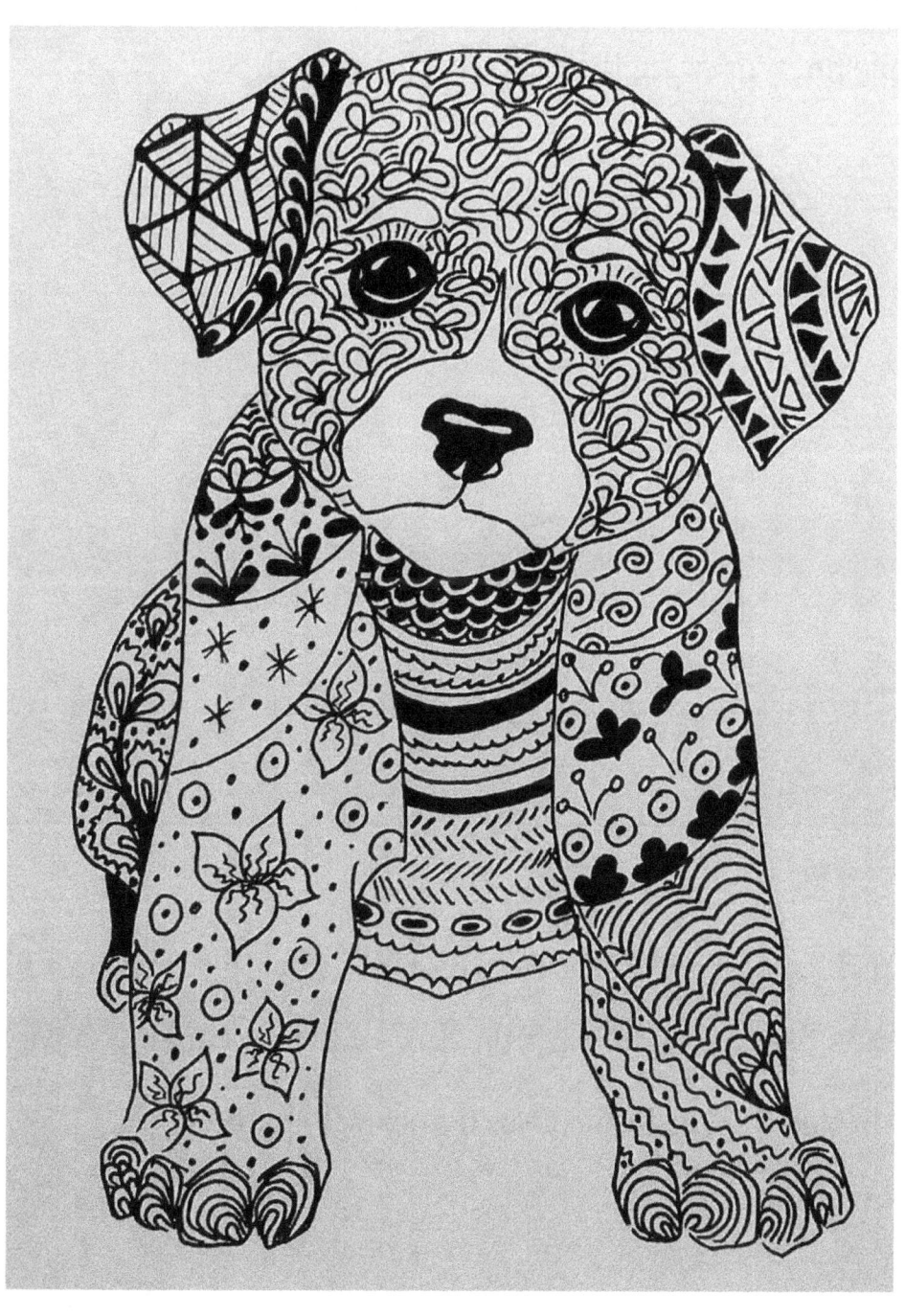

How to Draw a Crocodile?

Same as with the drawing of a puppy you should start with simple lines, drawing the shape of the animal.

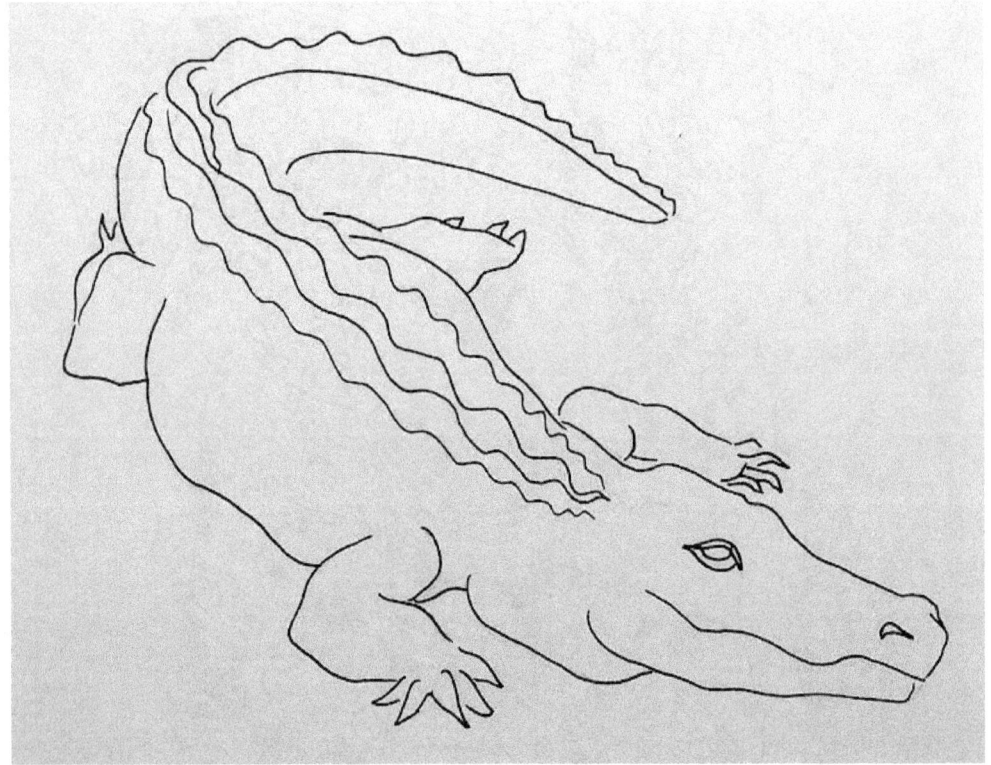

Now, you should let your mind go and draw whatever ornaments it wants to draw. Start with the tail. In the example, you can see that in this step, a simple, round lines will do the job.

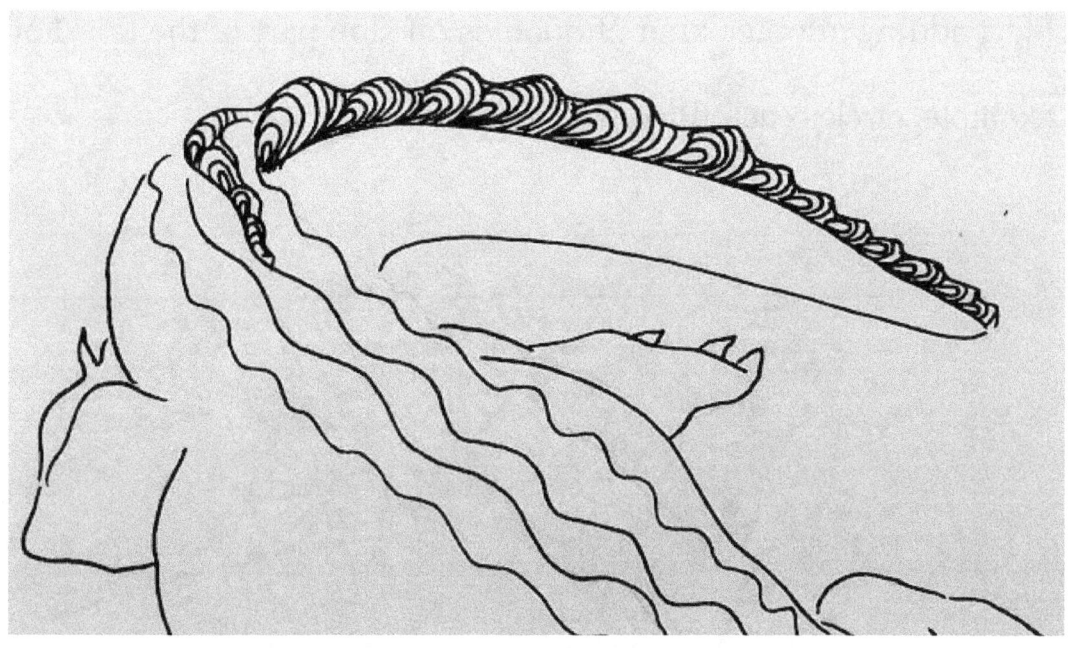

From tail move along the back line.

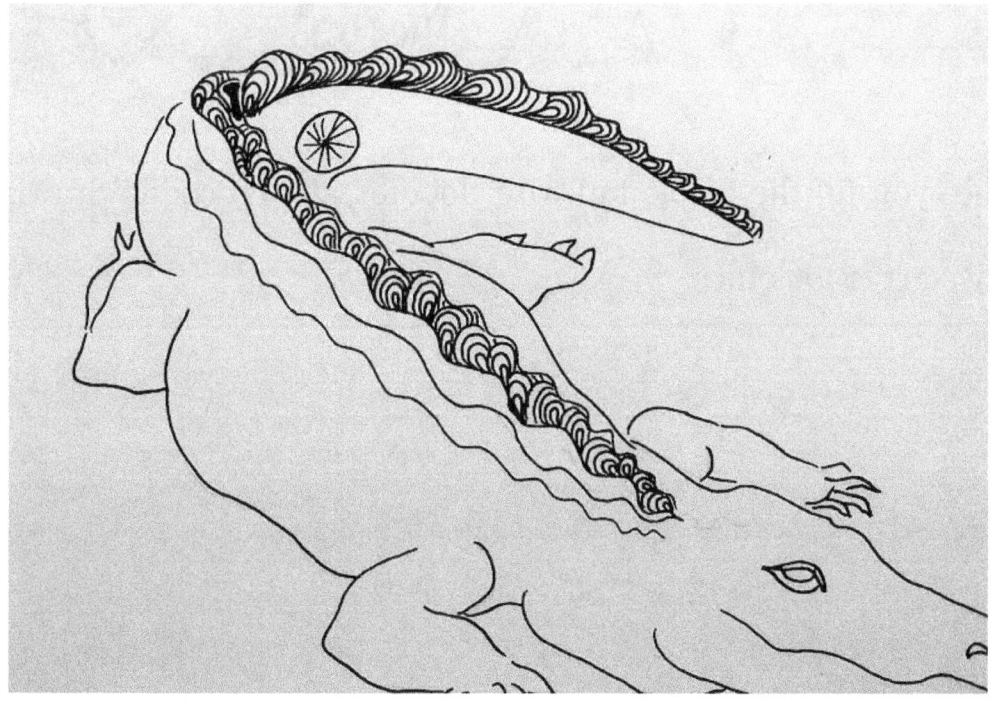

Start adding another kind of doodles on side part of the tail. For example, circles each filled with a snowflake.

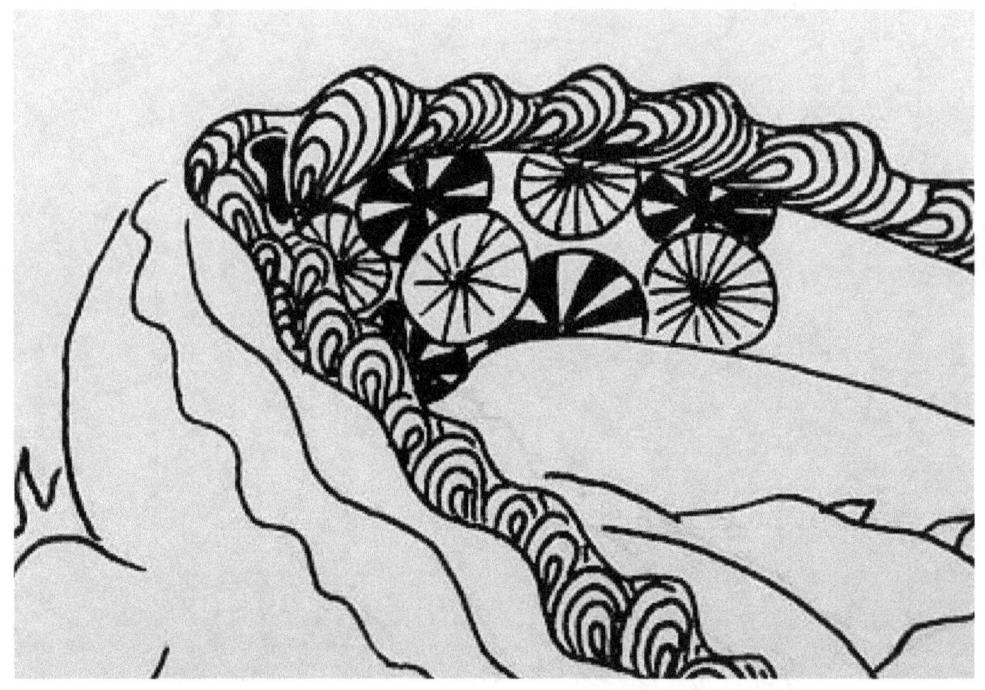

Once you fill the whole tail with doodles, the crocodile drawing will start to look nice.

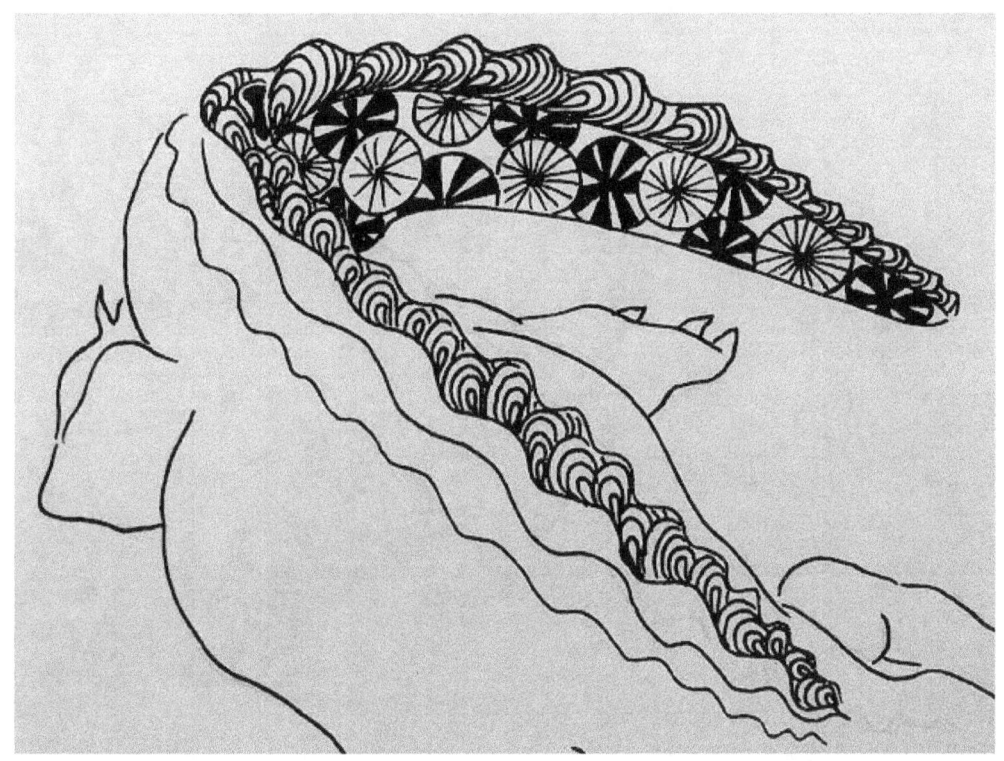

Add more doodles of different sort sideways to the back line. You can make this area darker, by drawing thicker lines or, in this case, filling the area.

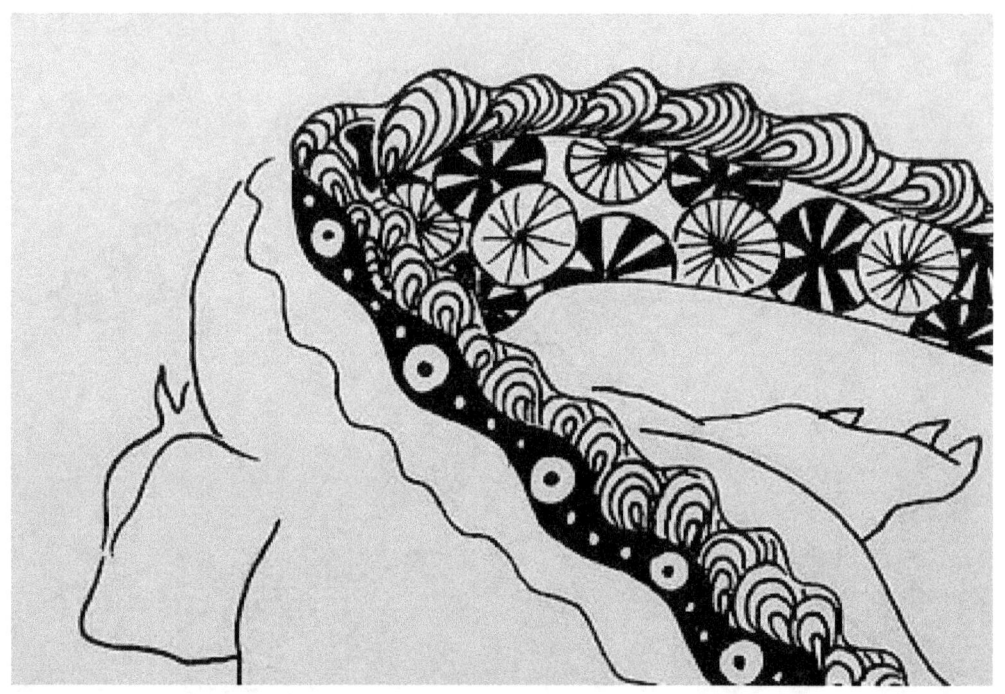

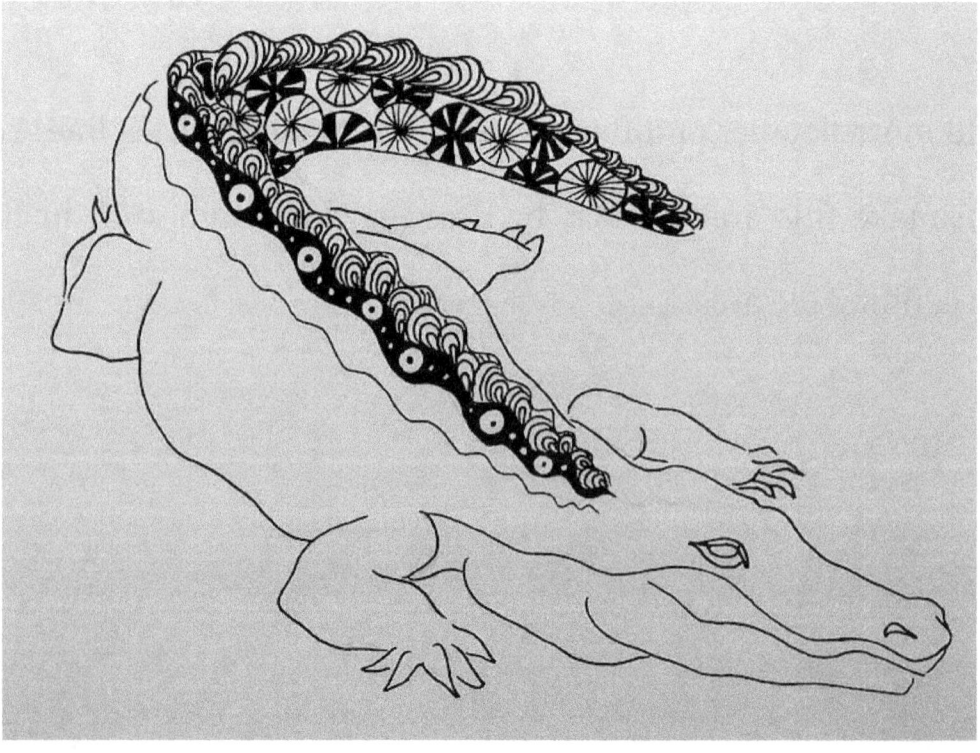

Draw new kinds of doodles on its back legs.

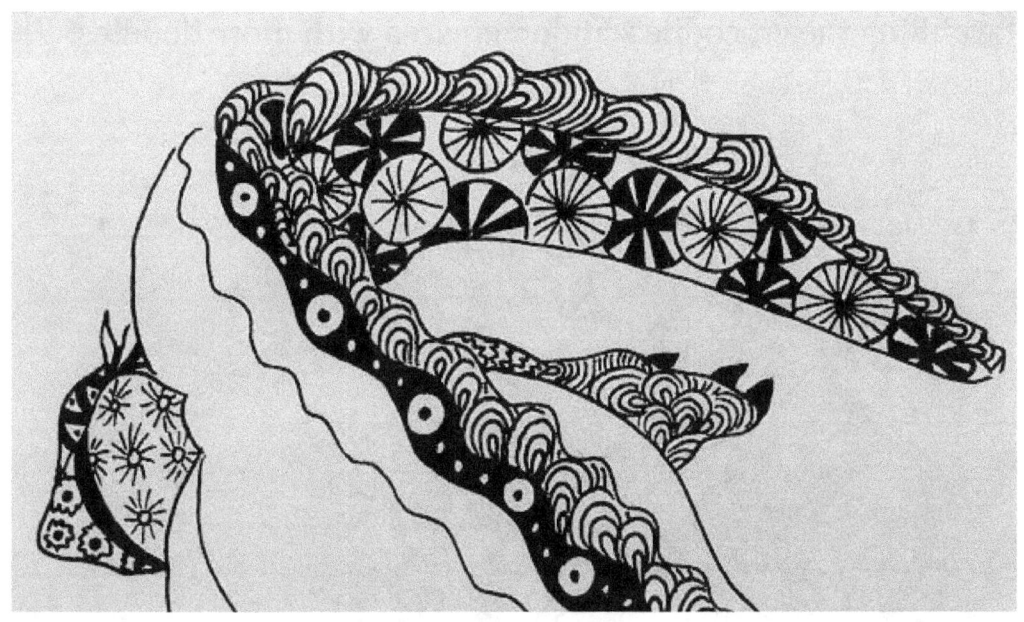

Add more lines to the center of its back.

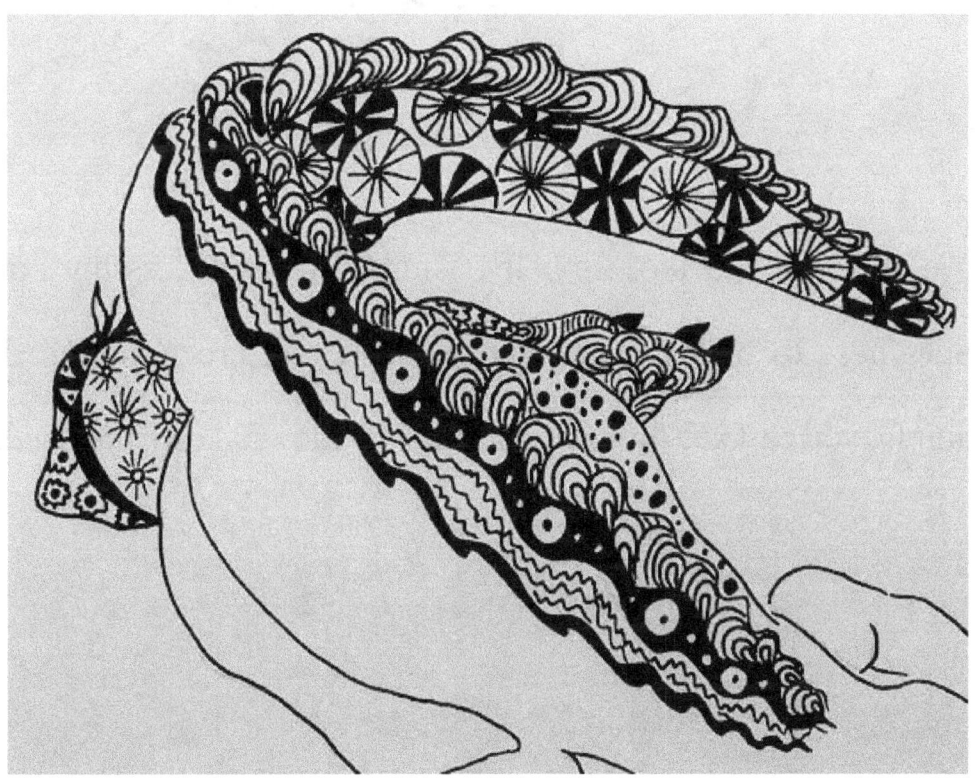

Start filling the crocodile's abdomen area with more doodles.

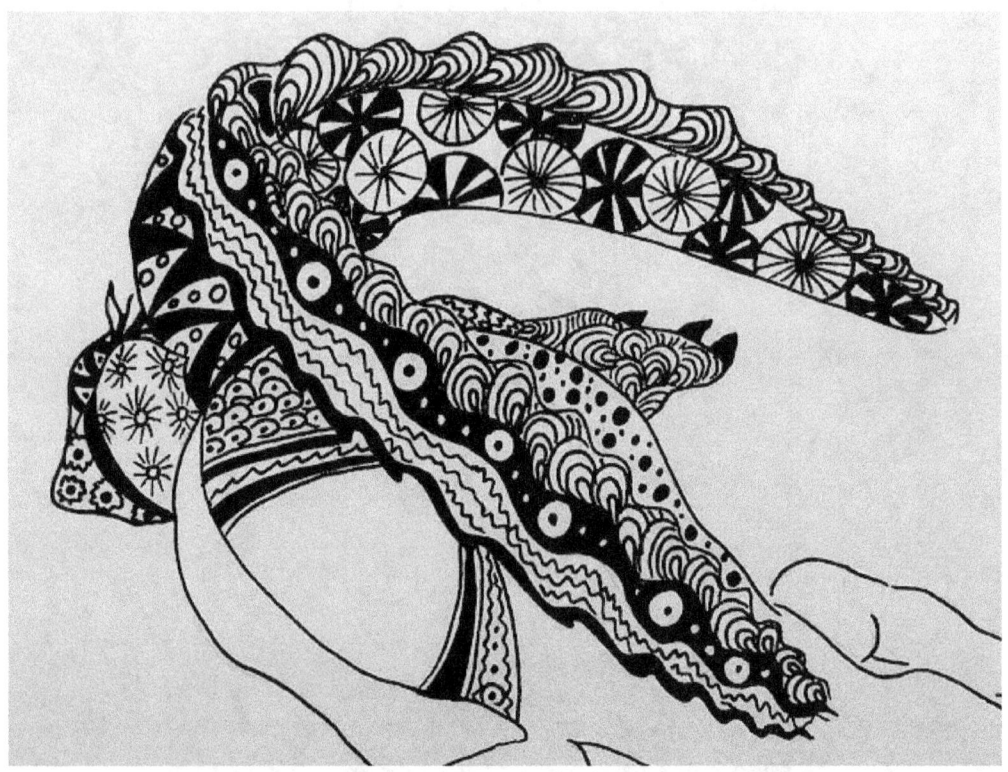

Move on to the sides of its belly. You can go with less lines and shapes here to make it look more like a real crocodile. In this example, you can see only small dots and snowflakes were used.

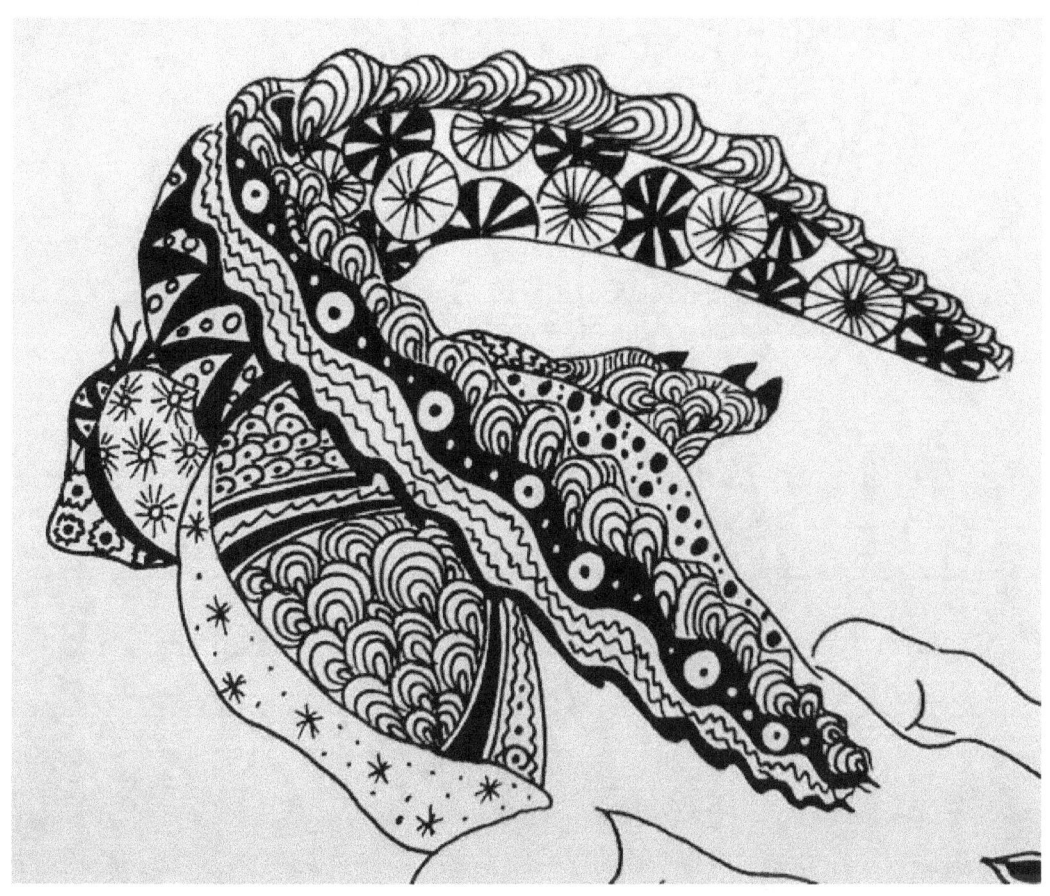

Start drawing doodles on a crocodile's front leg. You can go with

rhombuses this time.

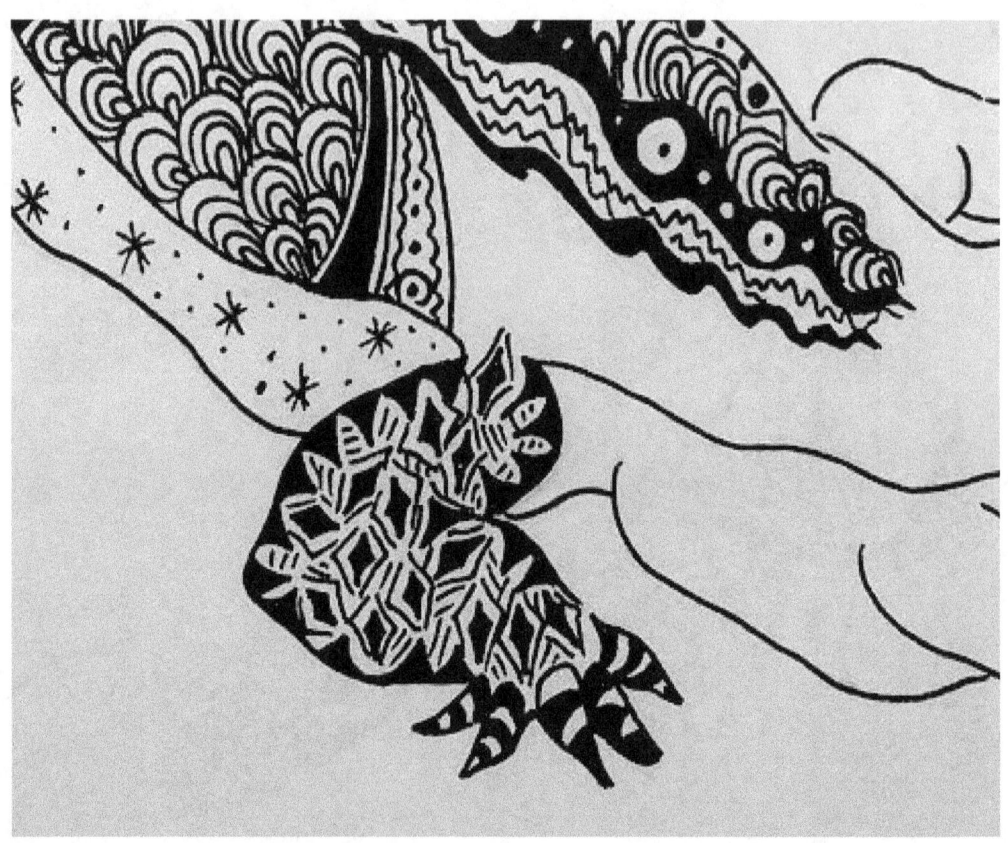

Do both front legs and the mandible. You could do the jaw in the

same manner as the belly.

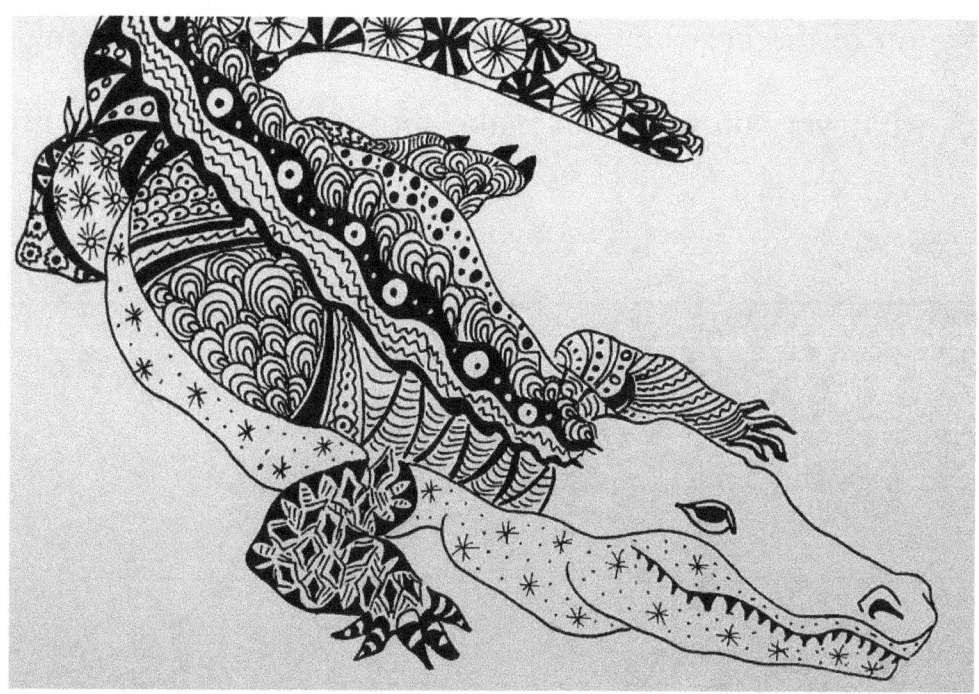

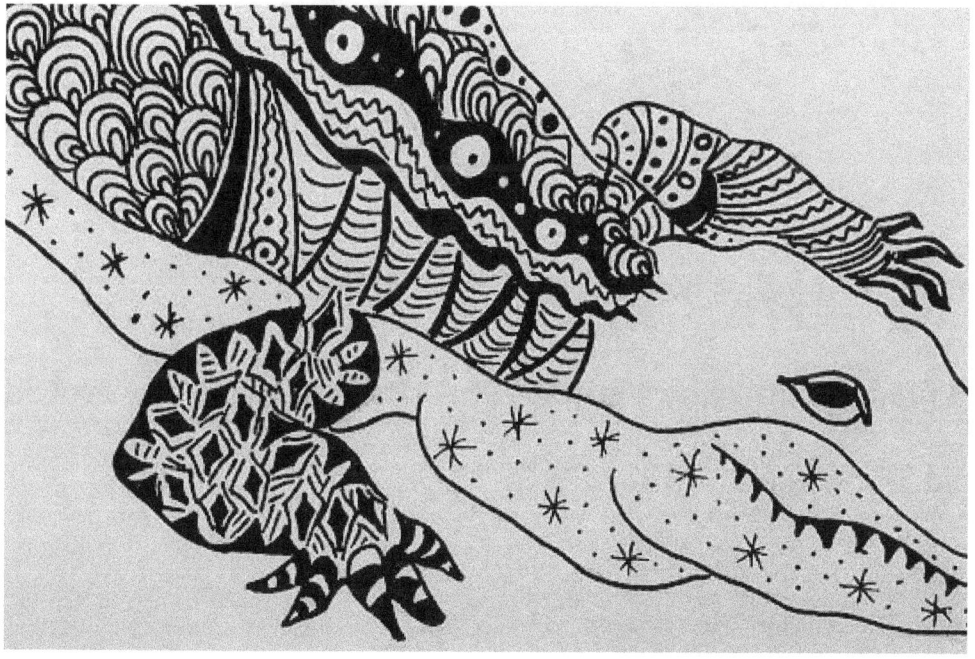

Move on to the head and draw Zen Doodles there – rectangles, dots, whatever you wish, but make sure they don't differ quite a lot.

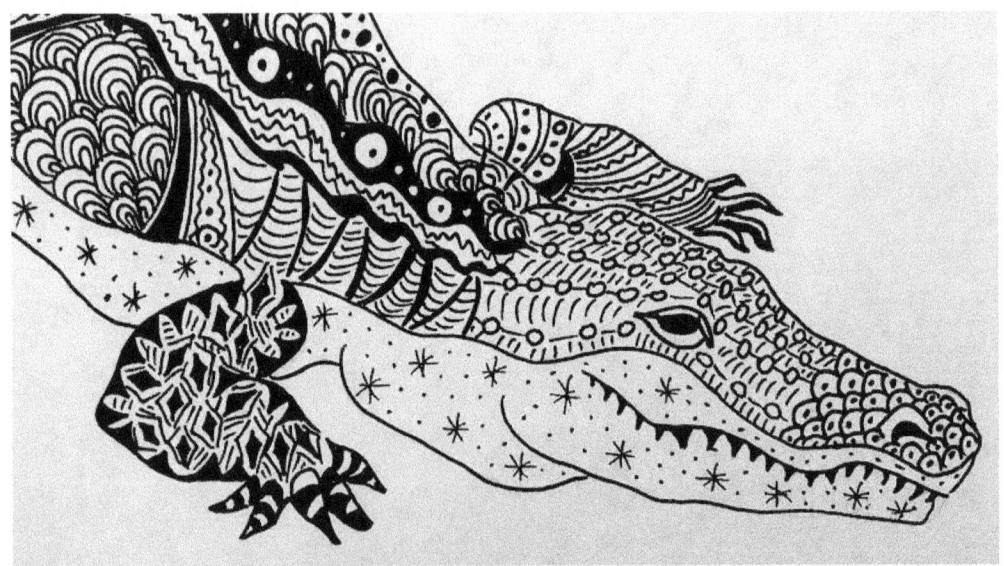

Finally, do doodles in areas that you find empty.

The final picture shows how a Zen Doodle drawing of a crocodile should look like.

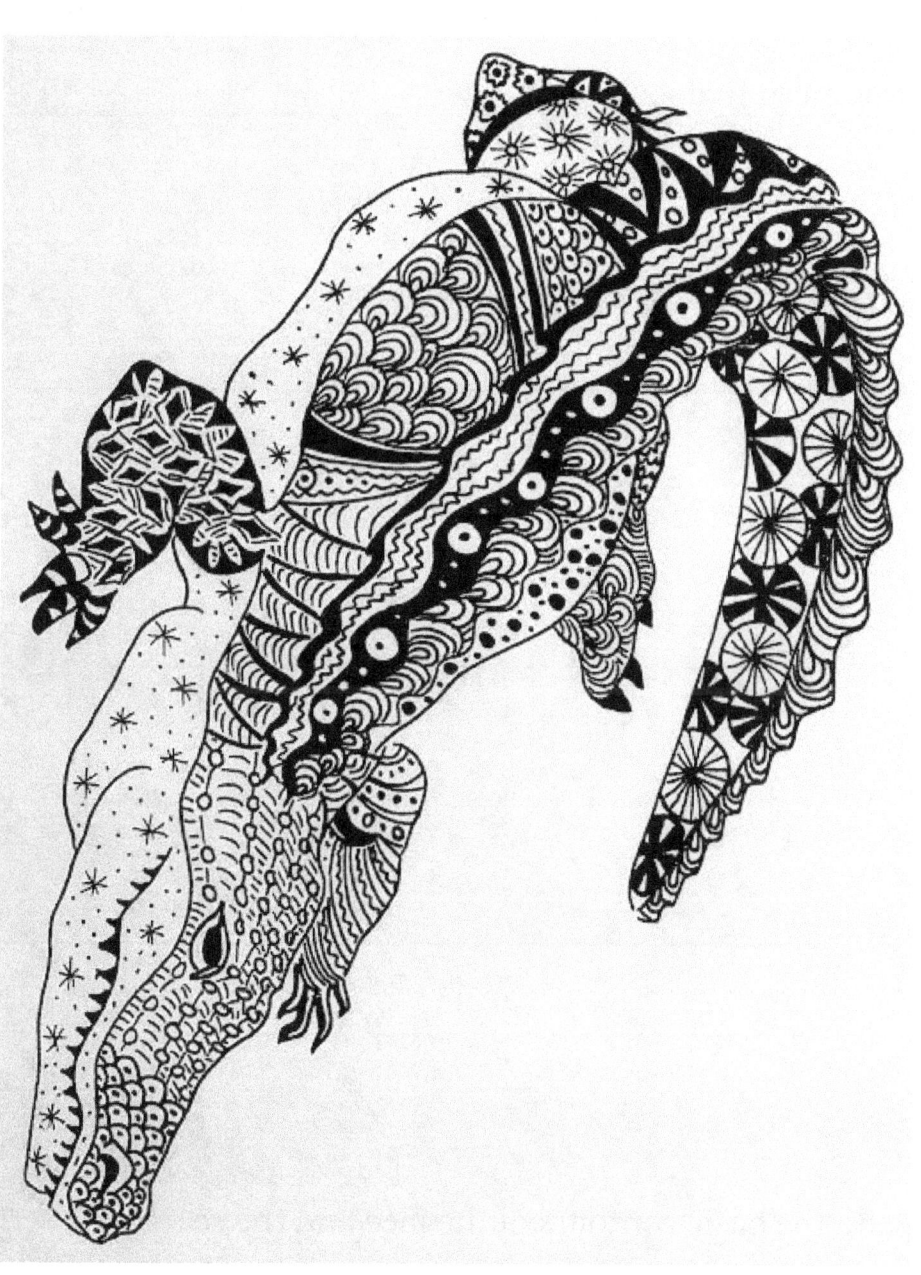

How to Draw a Girl Wearing a Scarf?

Remember this as a sort of rule – every time you start drawing a face, you need to do eyes first.

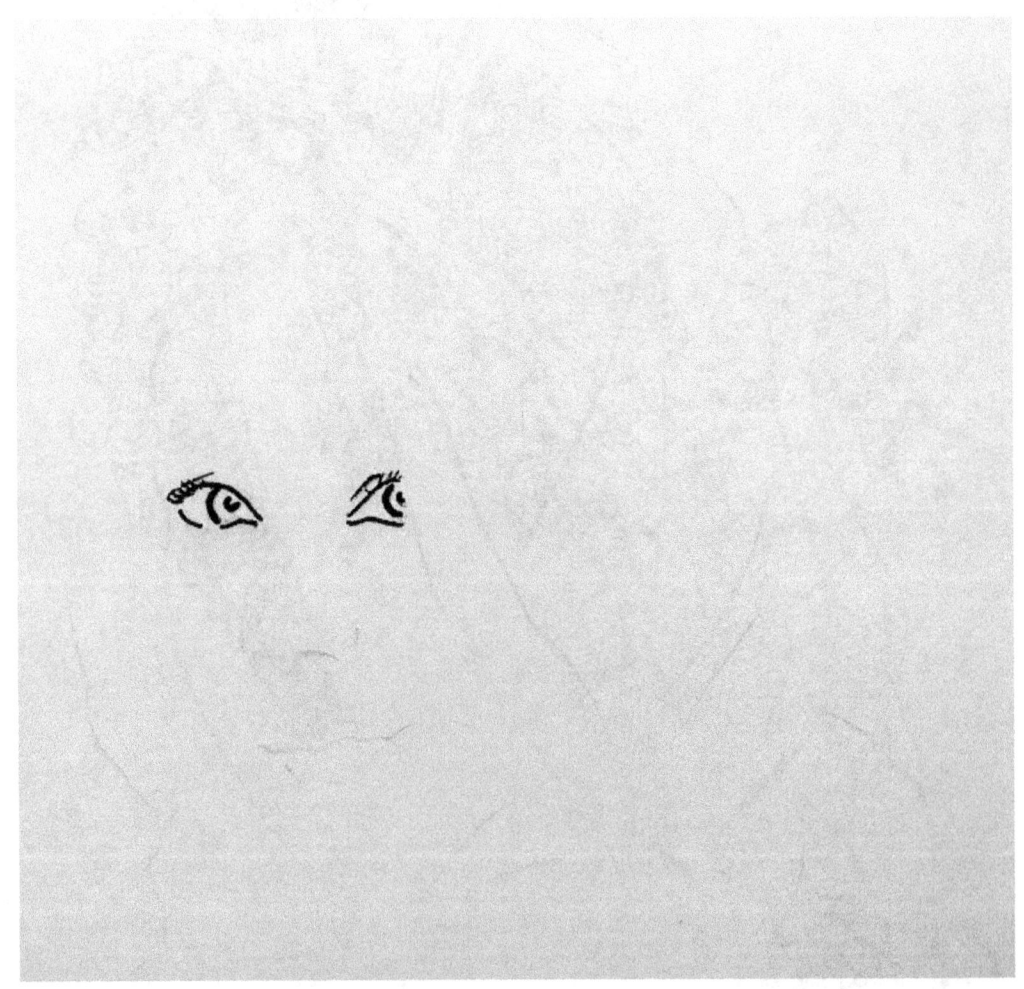

Now add the basic contours of the face and the scarf.

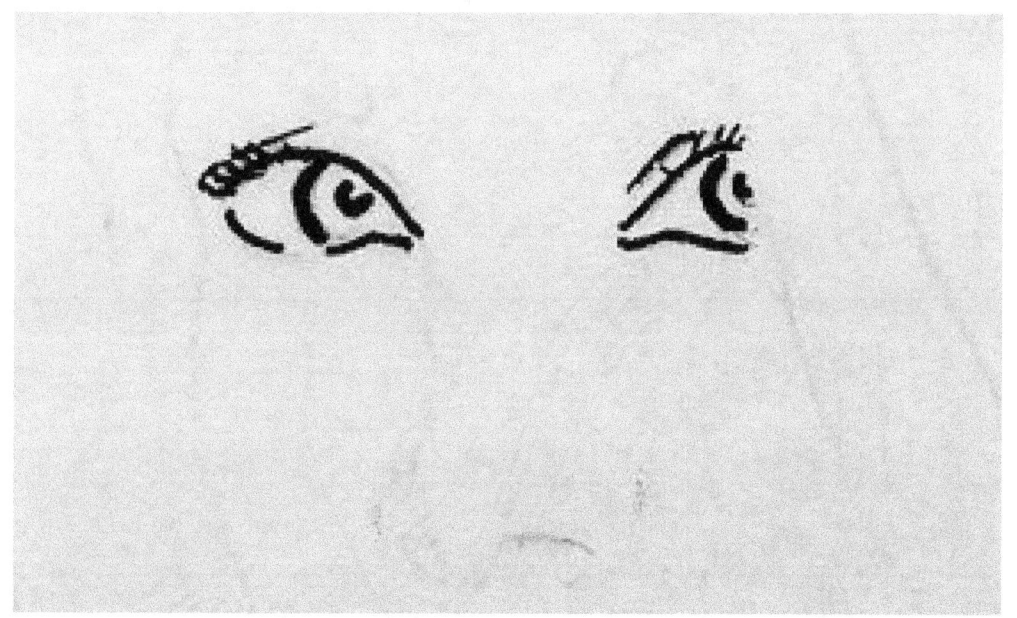

At this point, the eyes of the girl should be emphasized, while only thin lines should suggest the contours of the head.

Now, move onto drawing hair, nose and mouth.

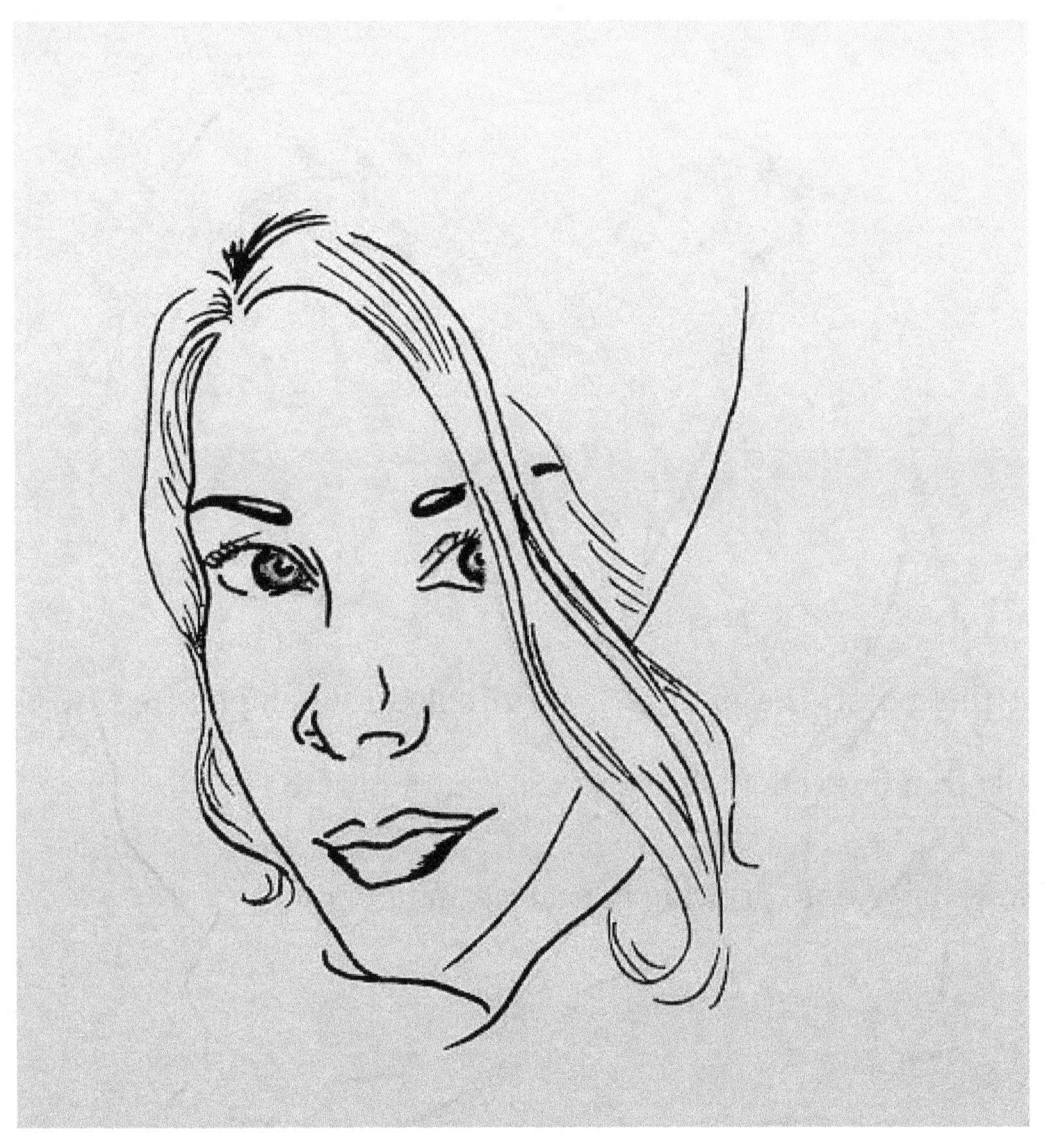

Bold the lines that make the head and the scarf, which you've previously sketched.

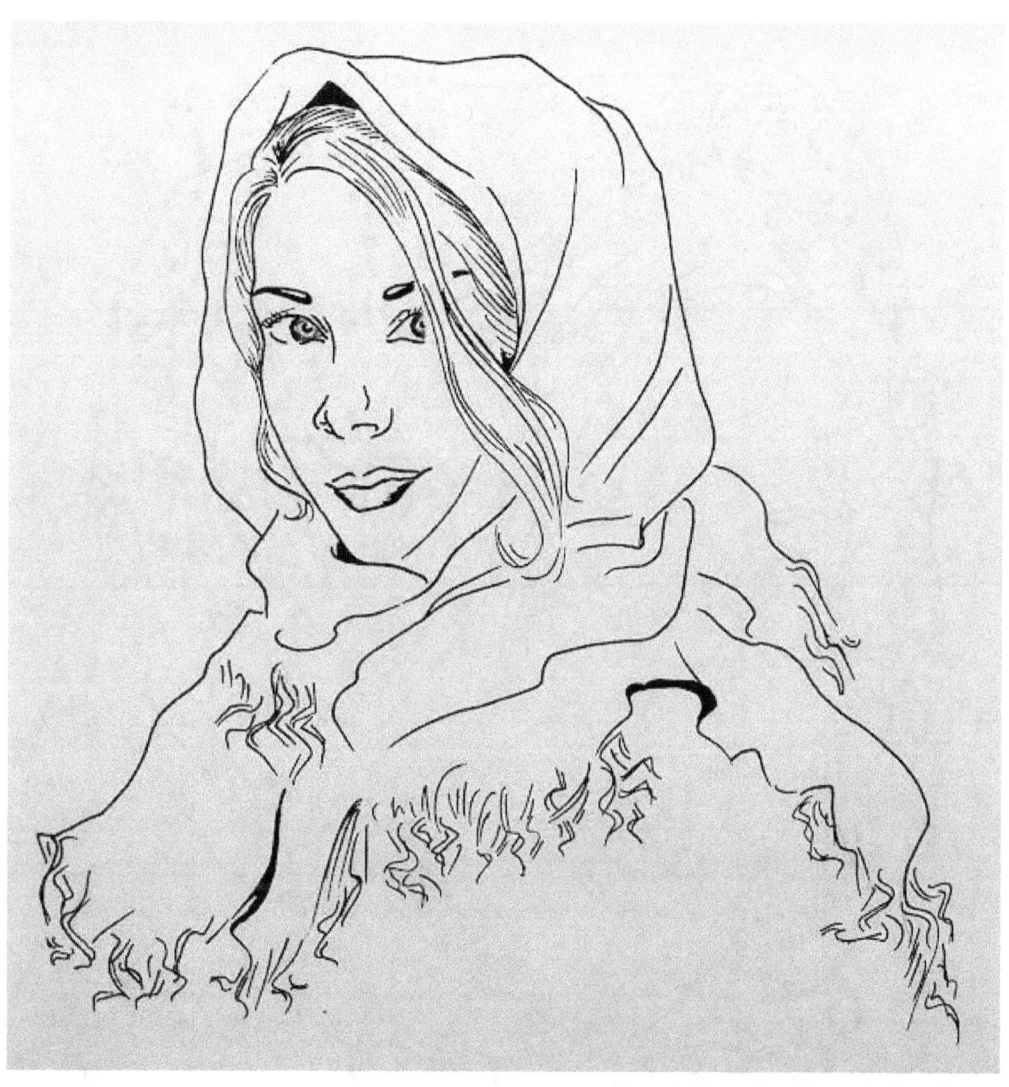

Focus on the scarf and start drawing doodles on it. You can go
with basic circles, flowers, etc. Make sure that scarf lines are the
borders that separate different styles of doodles.

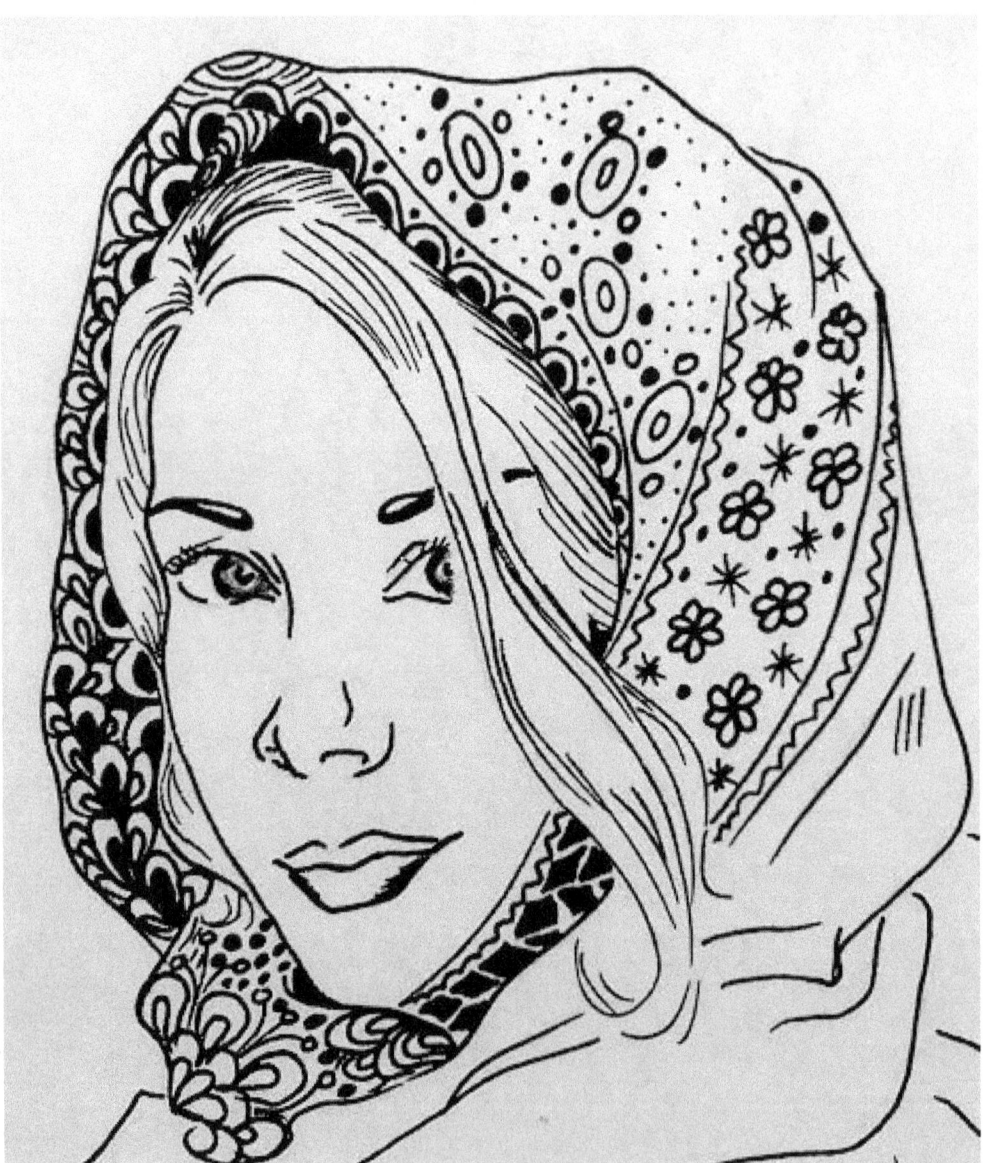

Try to cover the whole scarf with as many different types of ornaments as possible.

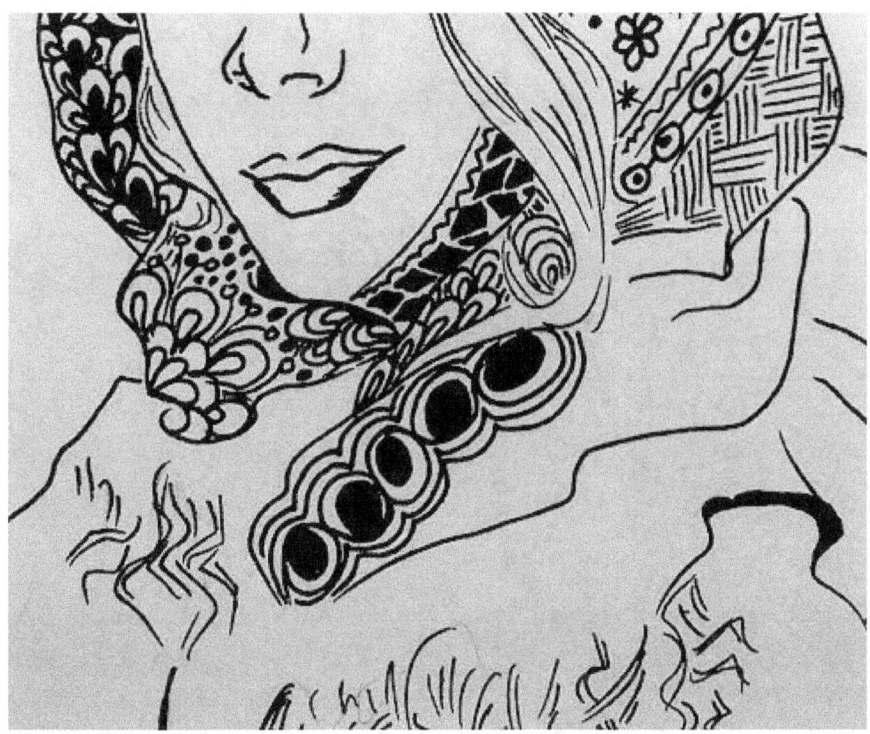

Focus now on the bottom side of the scarf, adding more doodles.

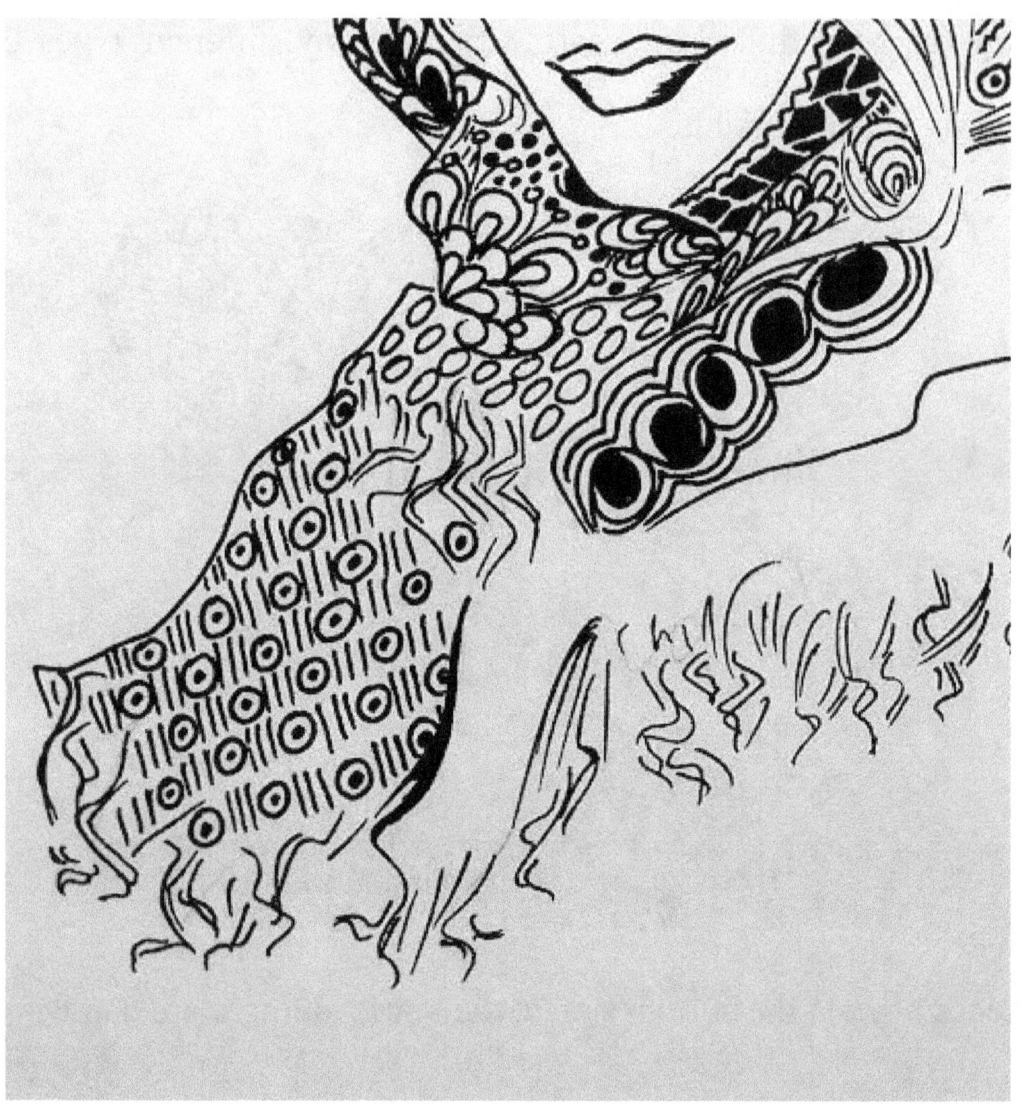

Keep on doodling until you cover the whole area. In this case, you can see many kinds of shapes, from points and circles to crescent moon.

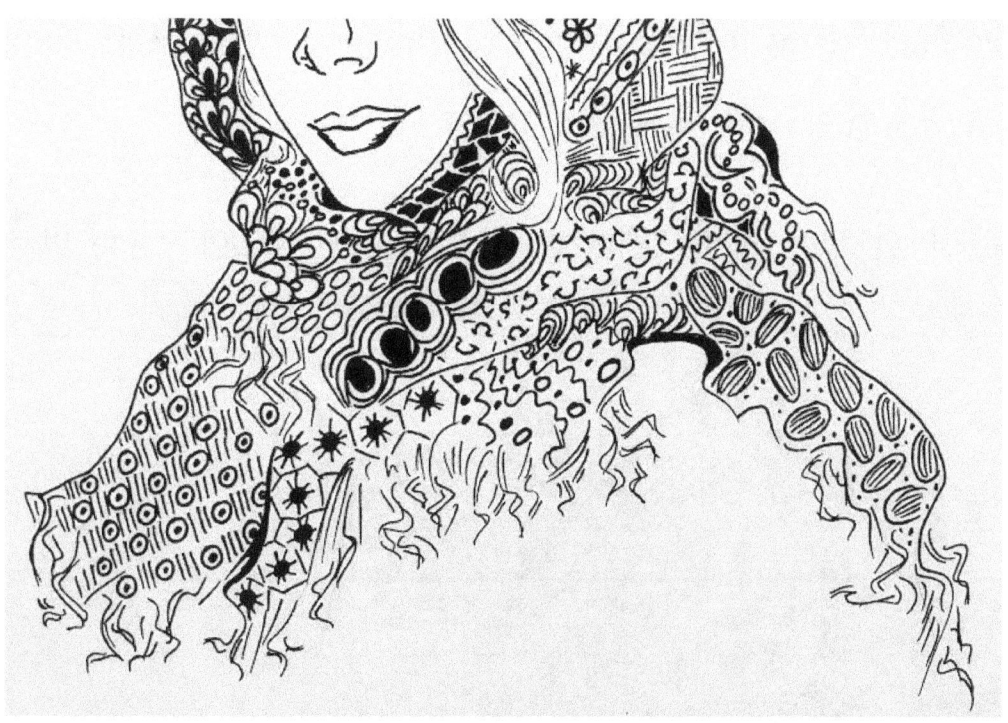

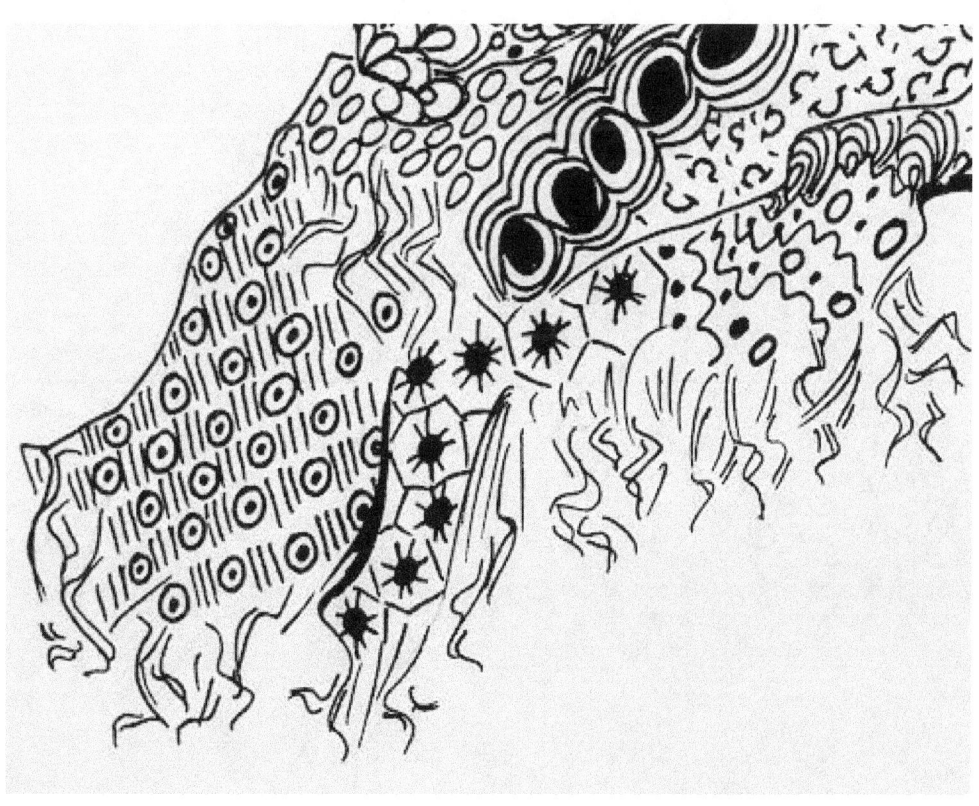

The final step is to look if there're some areas that seem empty and add ornaments there as well.

And this is how the final version of the drawing should look like.

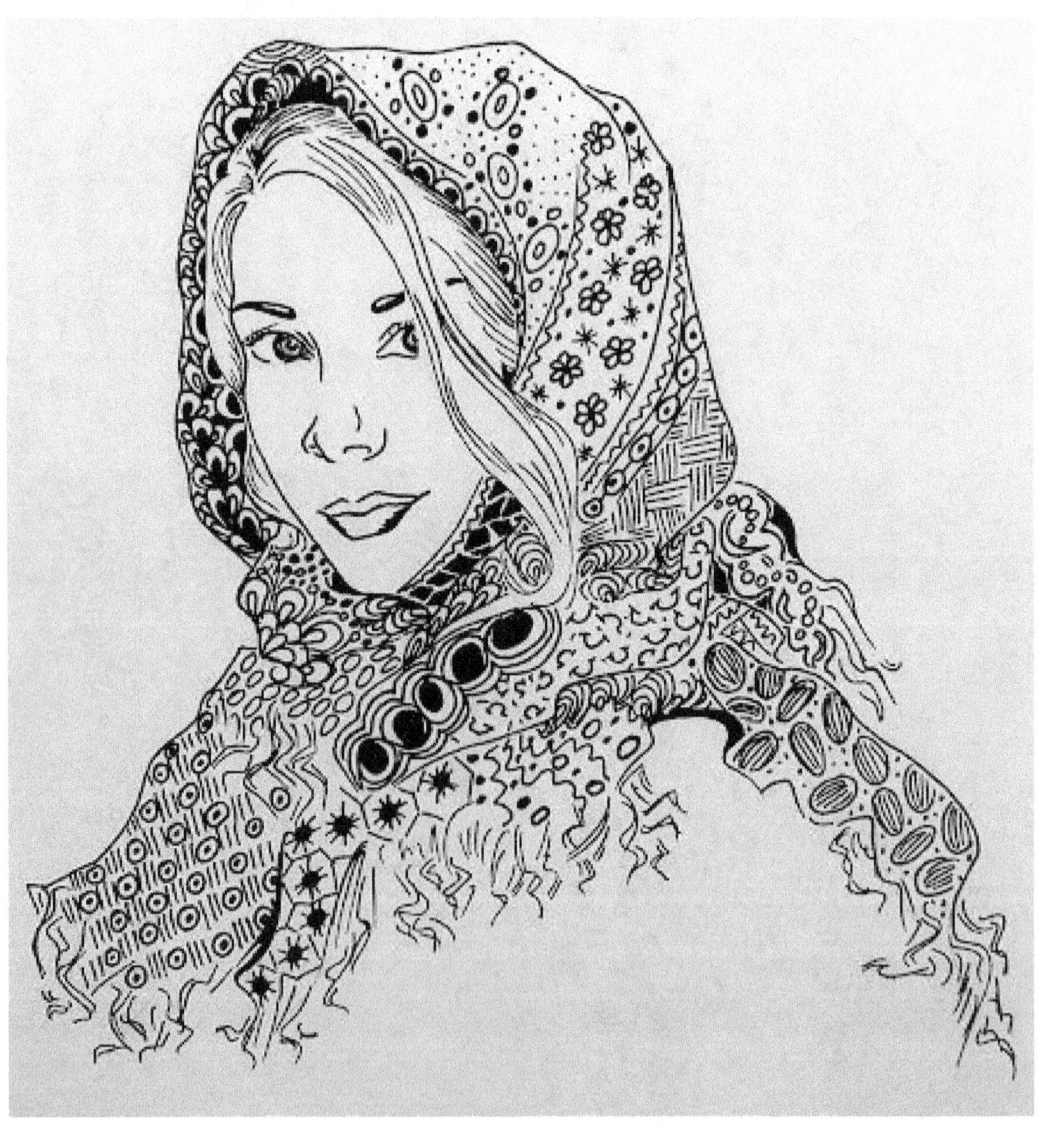

How to Draw a Swordfish?

Drawing a swordfish and Zen Doodling over it seems as a great way to produce an interesting work of art. First of all, the theme of the drawing is rather strange – you will not find many drawings of swordfish out there. The second reason is that a swordfish drawing leaves a lot of room for Zen Doodle drawing. You can cover almost the whole body of the fish with Zen Doodle ornaments. The final reason is that, unlike other animals, swordfish and other fish alike will not look strange with Zen Doodle drawings, which will appear as fish sherd. Start with drawing its head.

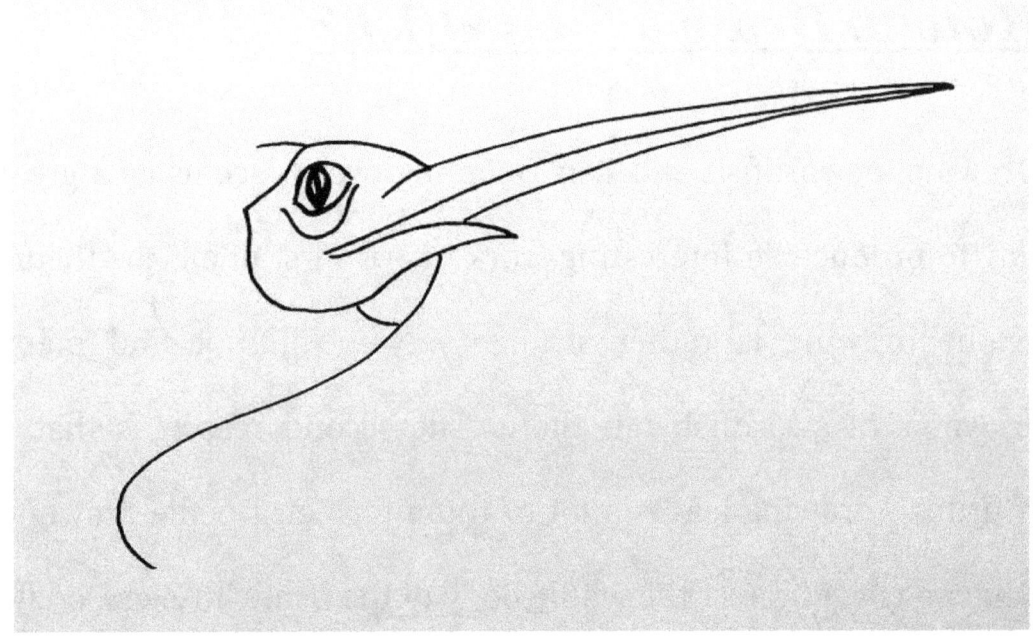

Add the back and side fins.

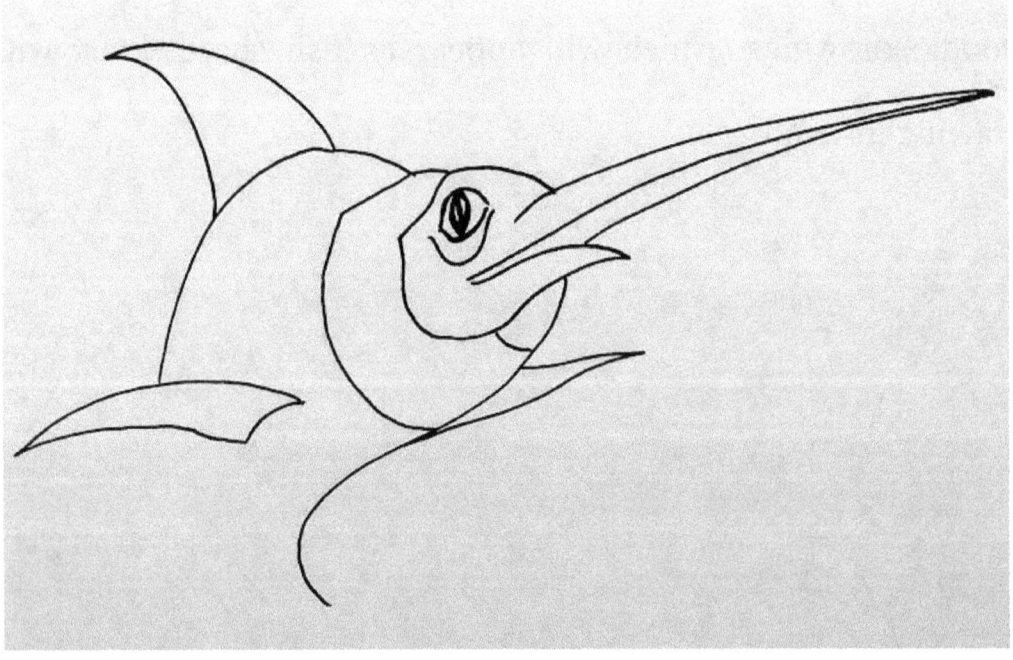

Draw the basic lines that will make the whole body of the fish.

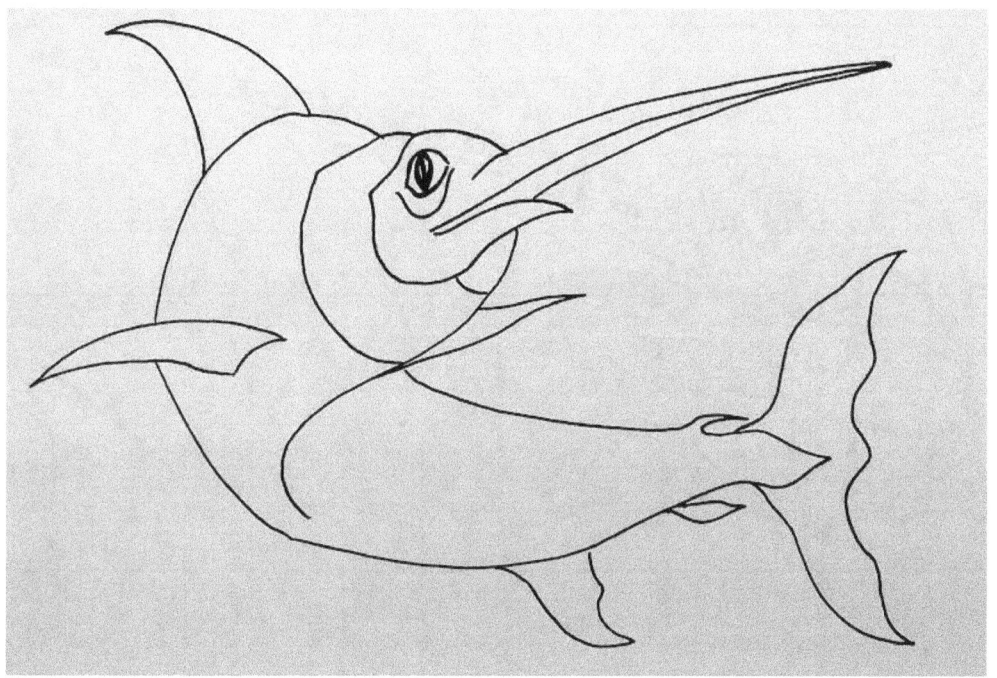

Start doodling from the nose, which is shaped like a sword. Why don't you emphasize it by drawing darker doodles?

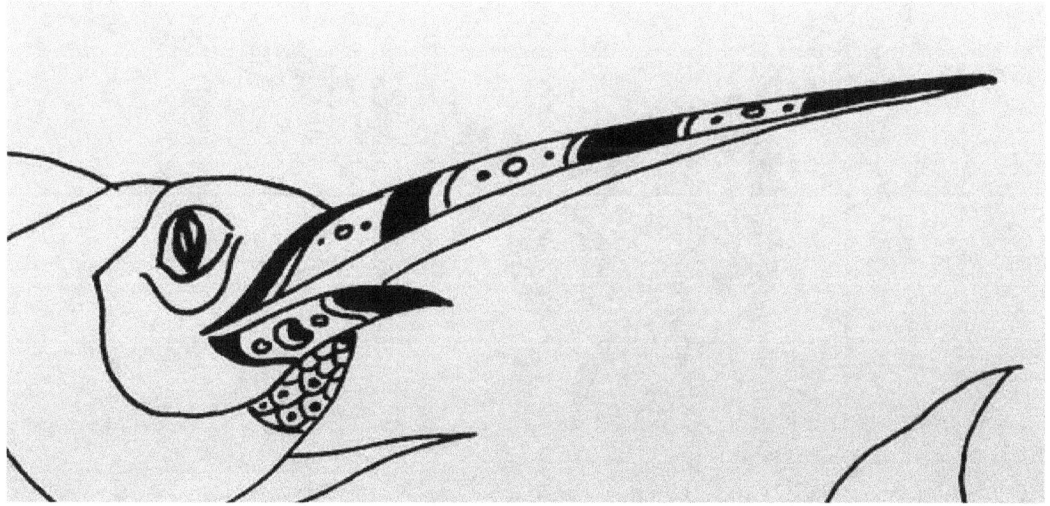

Move on to the head of the swordfish. Basic circles will do the job.

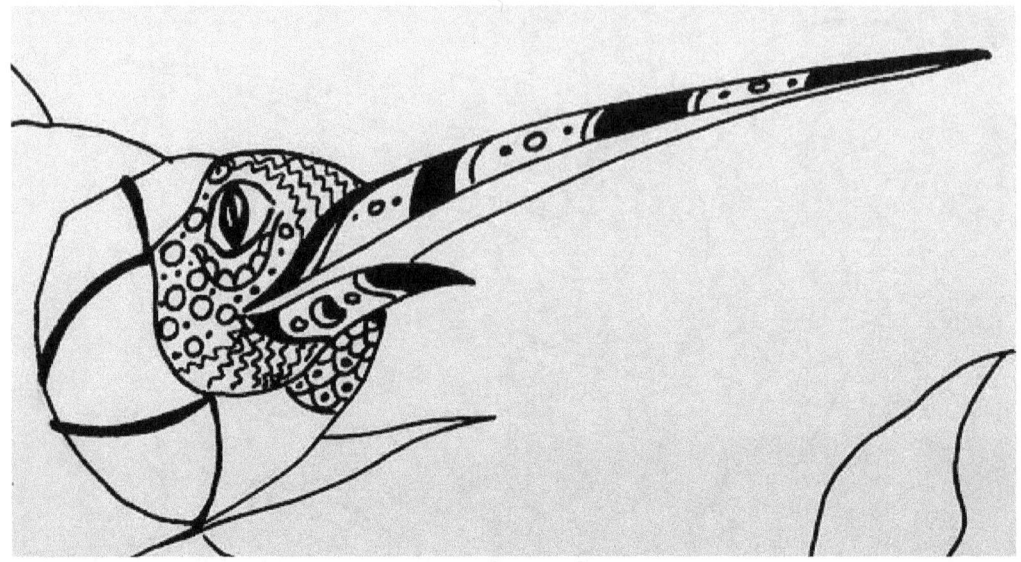

Once you're done with the head, you'll see where you should doodle next.

Finish the head and do the top fin.

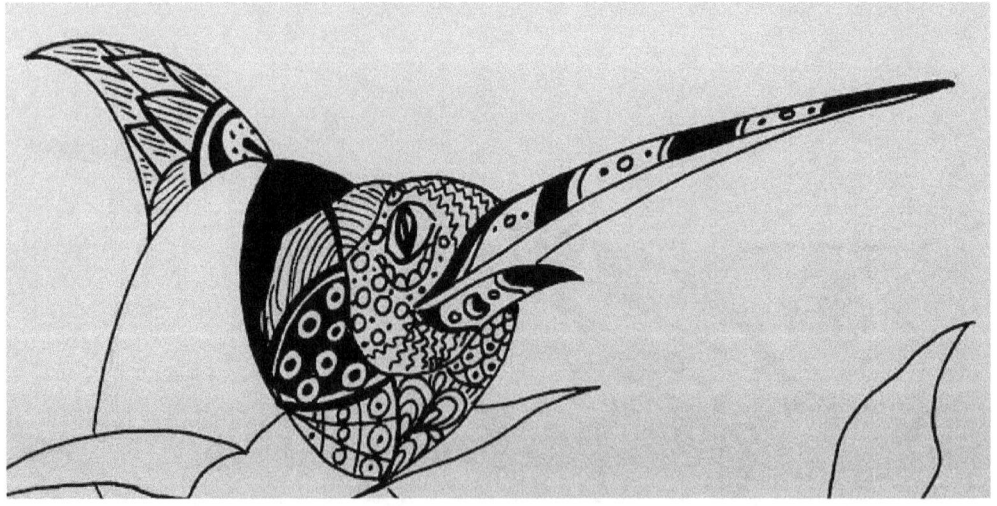

Start drawing doodles on the fish's body.

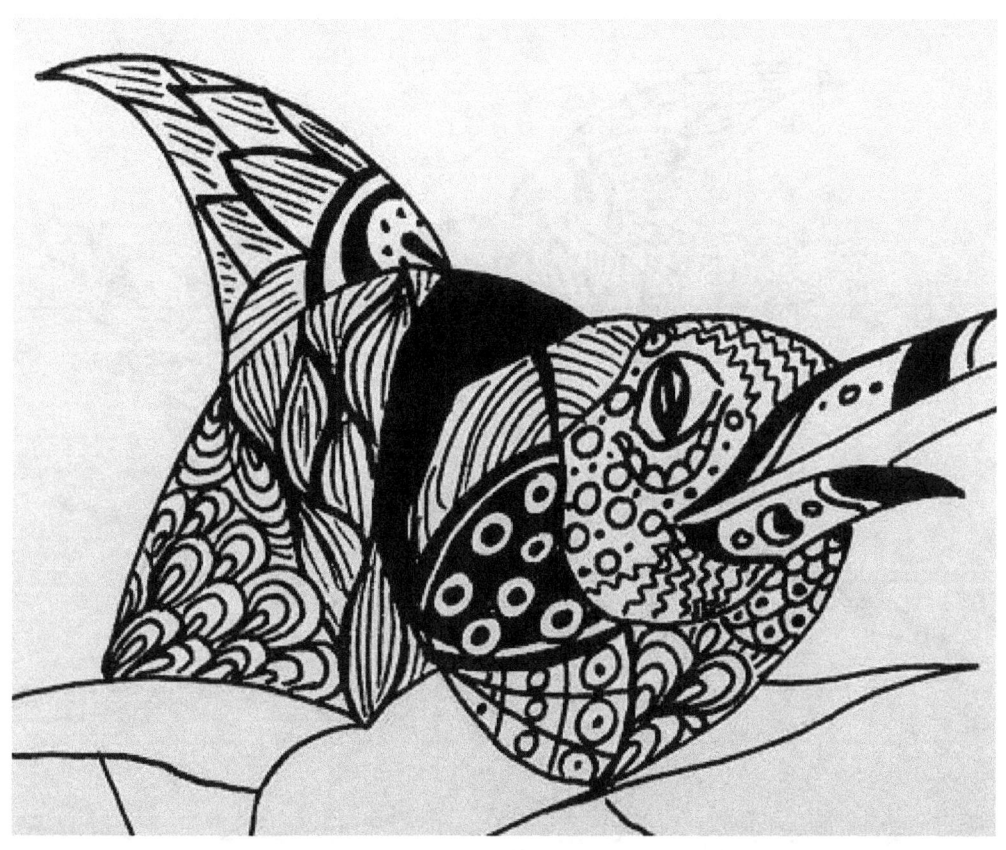

Draw along the back line. The pattern you could use are concentric semicircles.

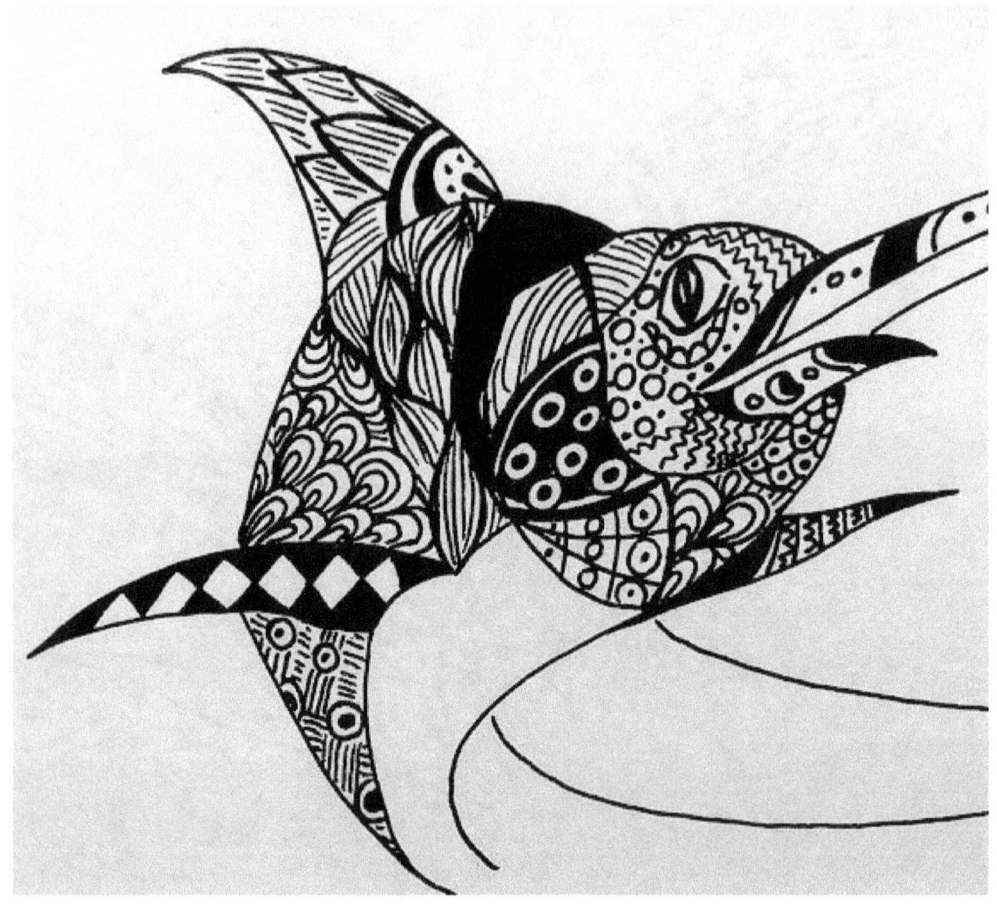

Do the whole back and draw doodles on the tail. The more patterns you use at this point, the final drawing will look more interesting. So, go with triangles, zigzag lines, and flowers.

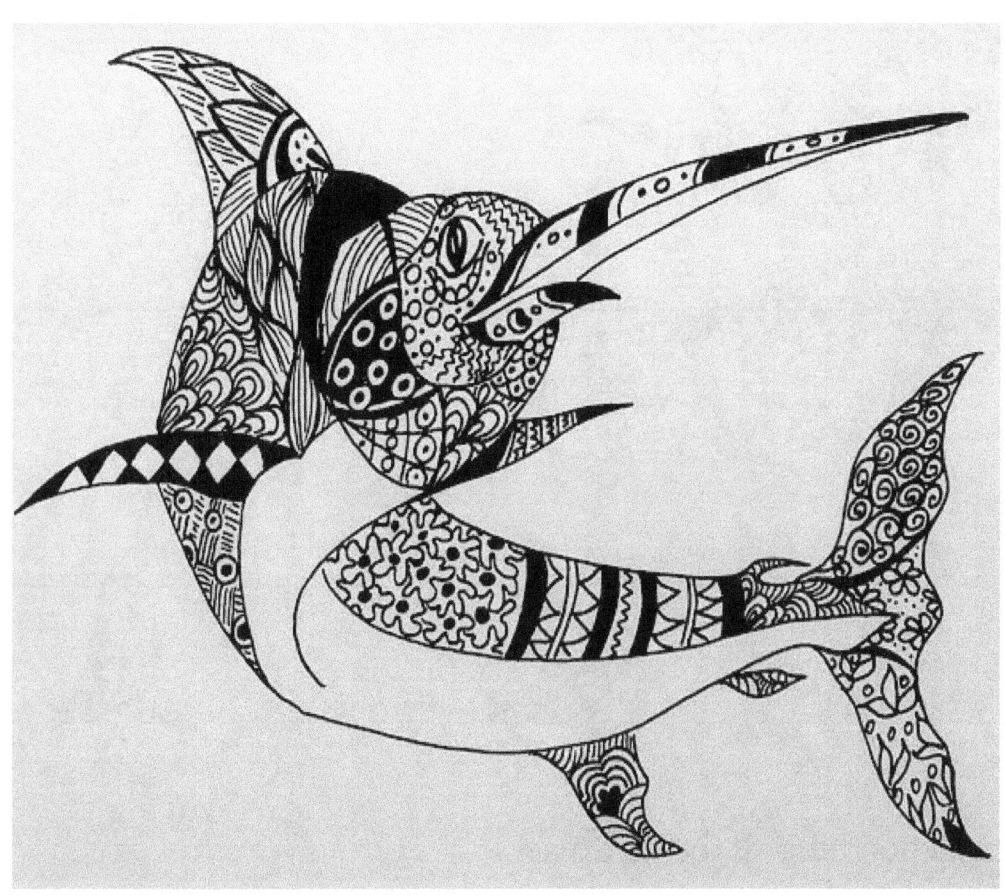

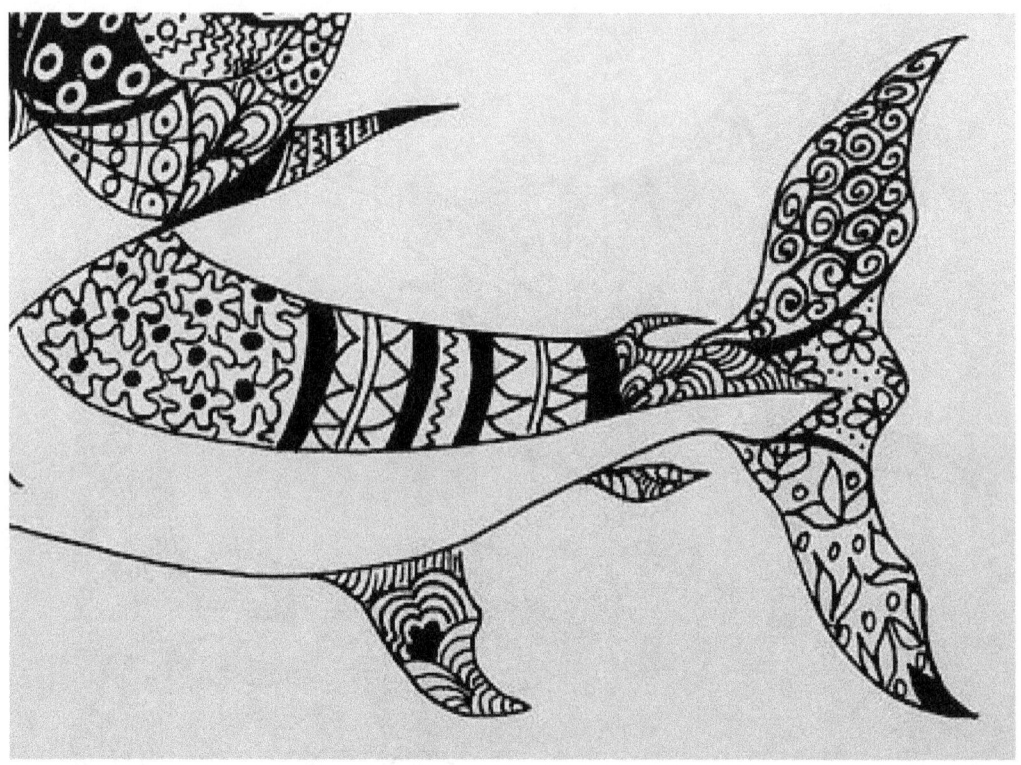

Finish doodling all the fin areas.

Try to do fill each fin area with a different pattern. In the case you see here, we used eight types.

The final step is to do the belly. As you can see in the example, this area should be covered with a smaller number of shapes. Use lines and circles, but not too much. This should be it – your drawing of a swordfish is complete

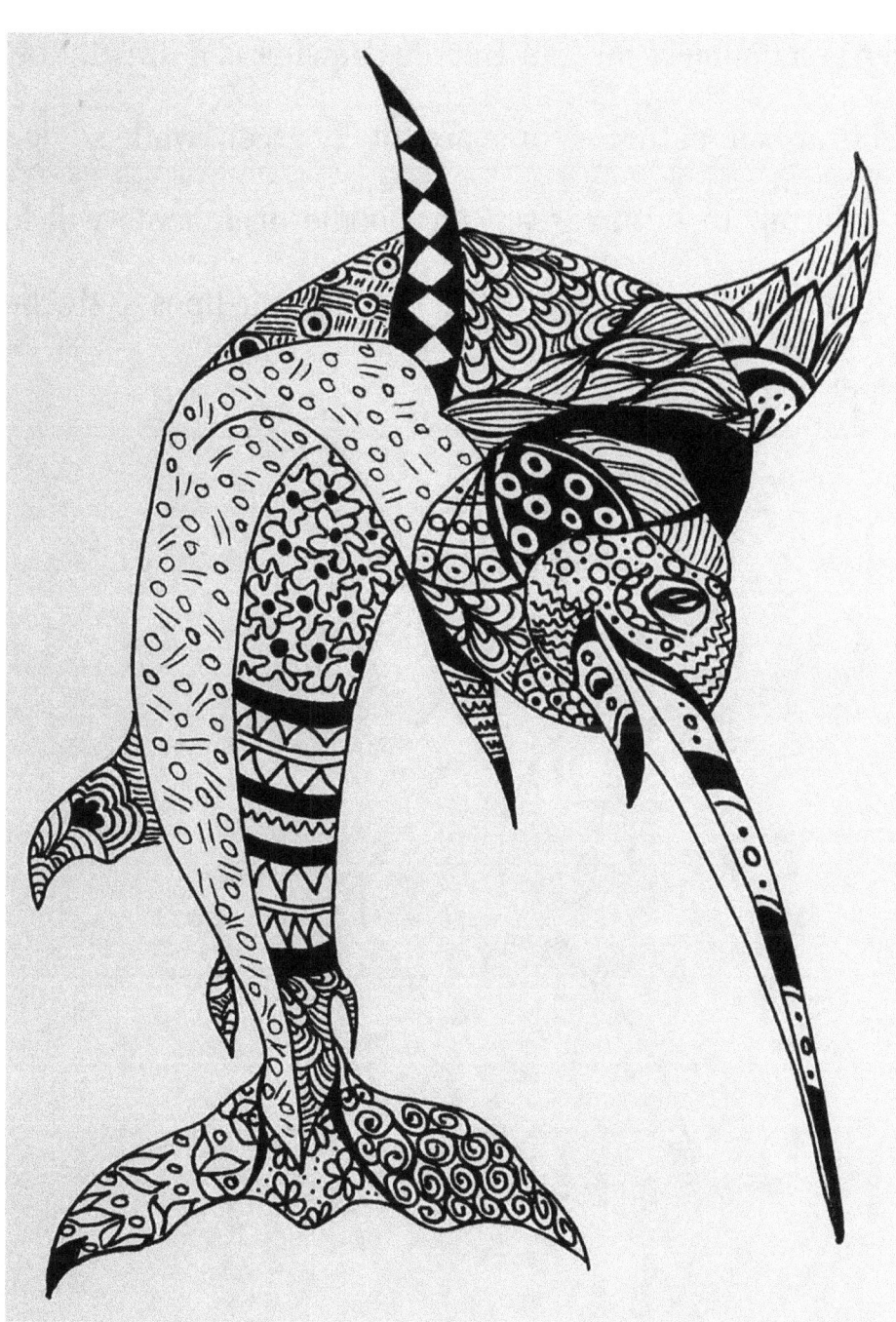

How to Draw a Lizard?

Another great subject for Zen Doodle drawing is a lizard. You've all seen lizards in nature – some are totally green, while some are pretty colorful. In both cases, Zen Doodle ornaments will look amazing on their bodies. Start with drawing the lines of the head and upper body.

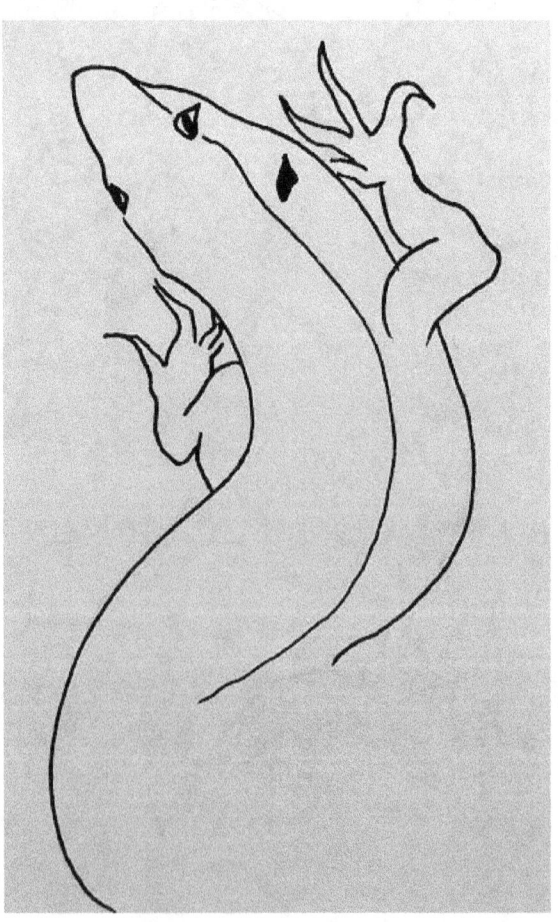

Move on to back legs and tail...

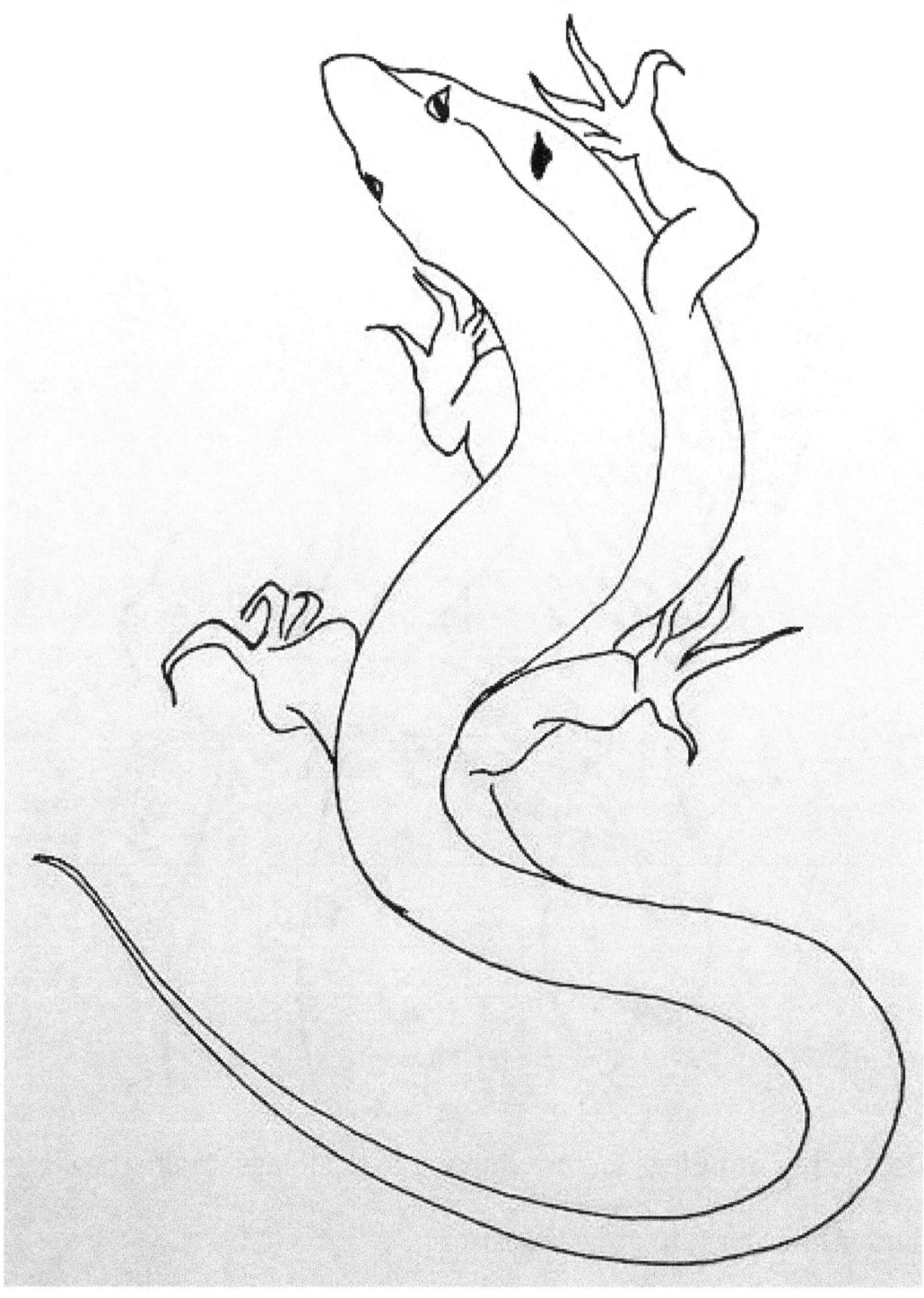

Start drawing ornaments on the lizard's head. Try to do each layer with a different pattern, from simply putting a few dots, to zigzag lines.

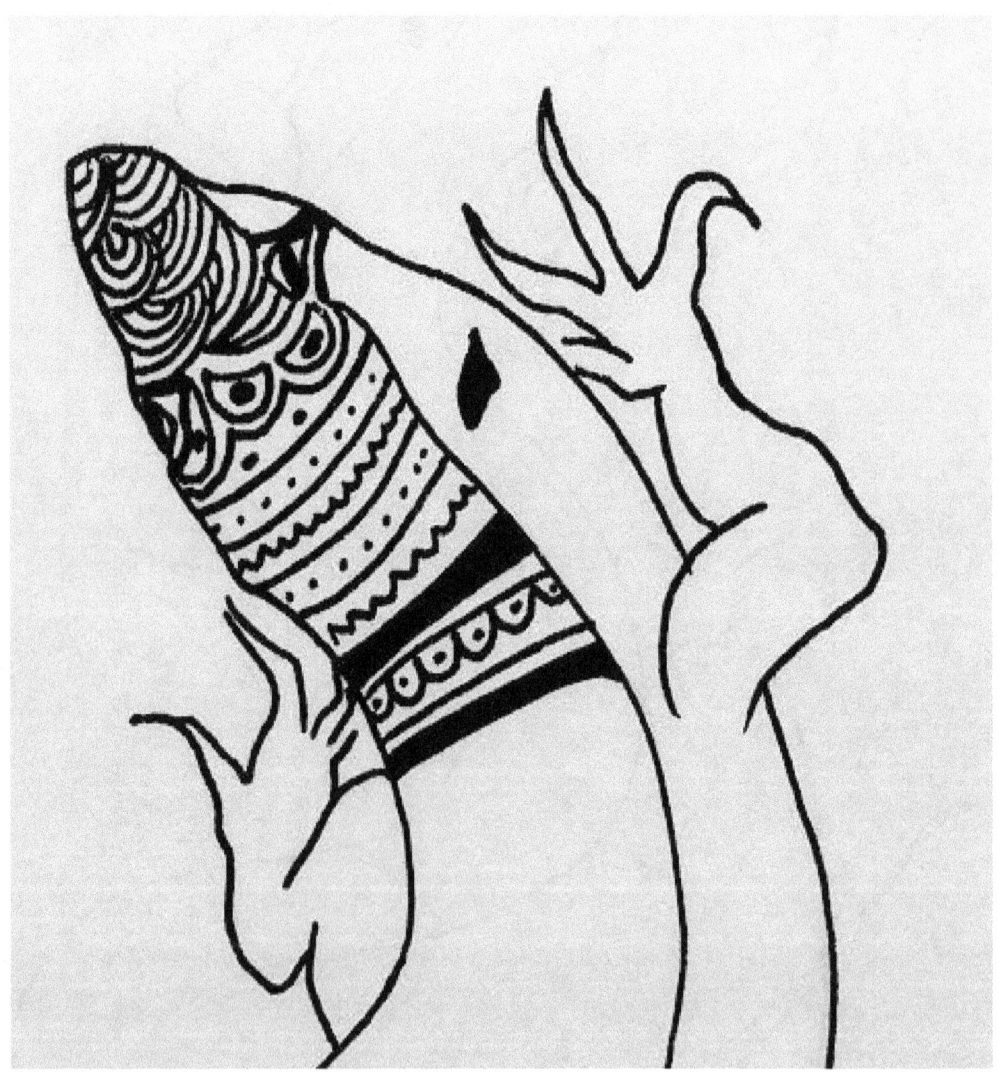

Doodle the front legs, before moving to back legs. Make the claws darker in order it to appear scarier.

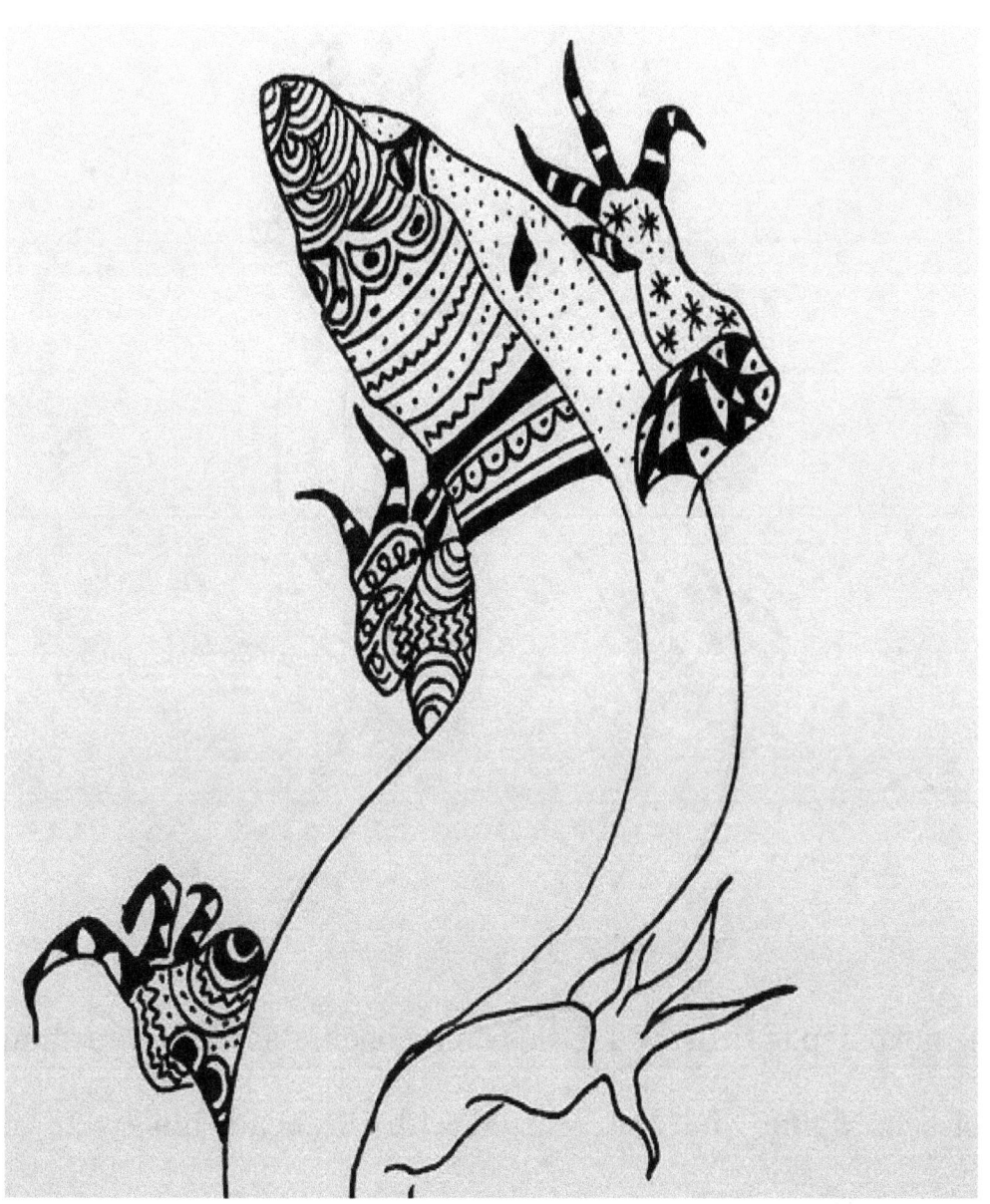

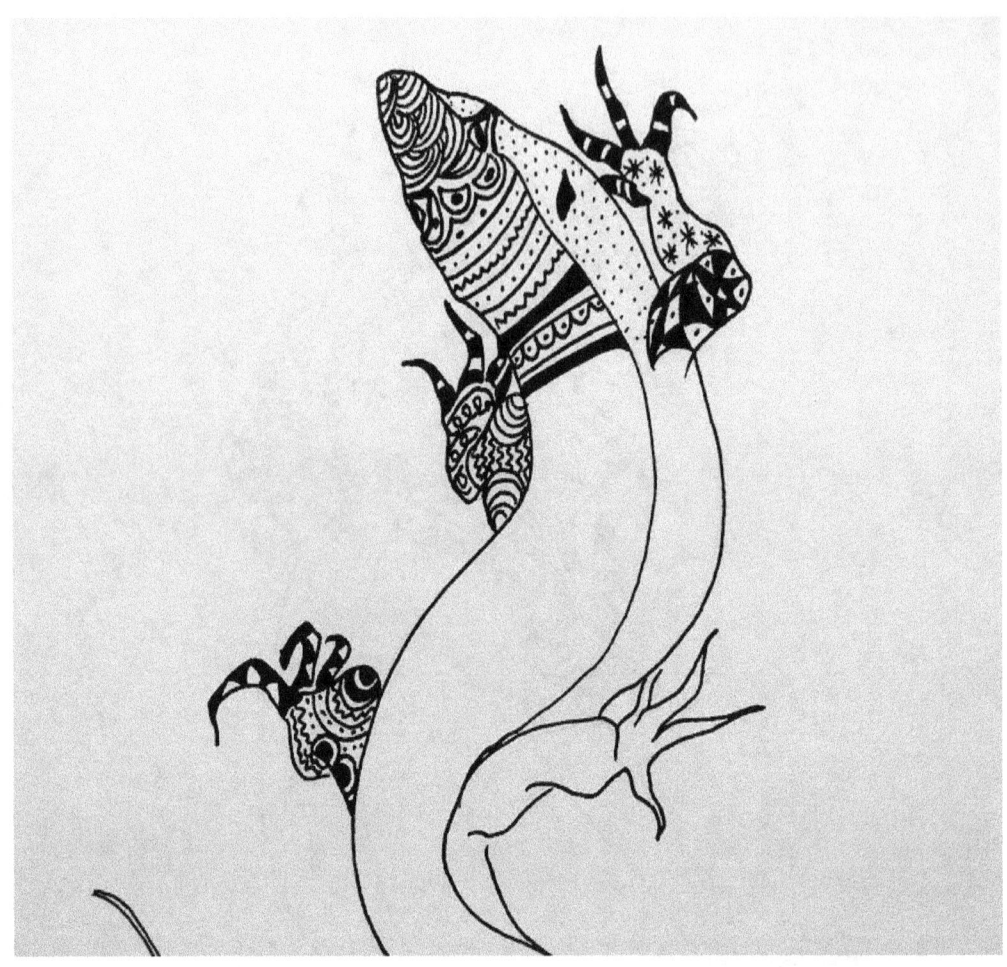

The next step is to draw doodles on its back. Basically, you should just keep doing what you started with the head, but try to add more patterns.

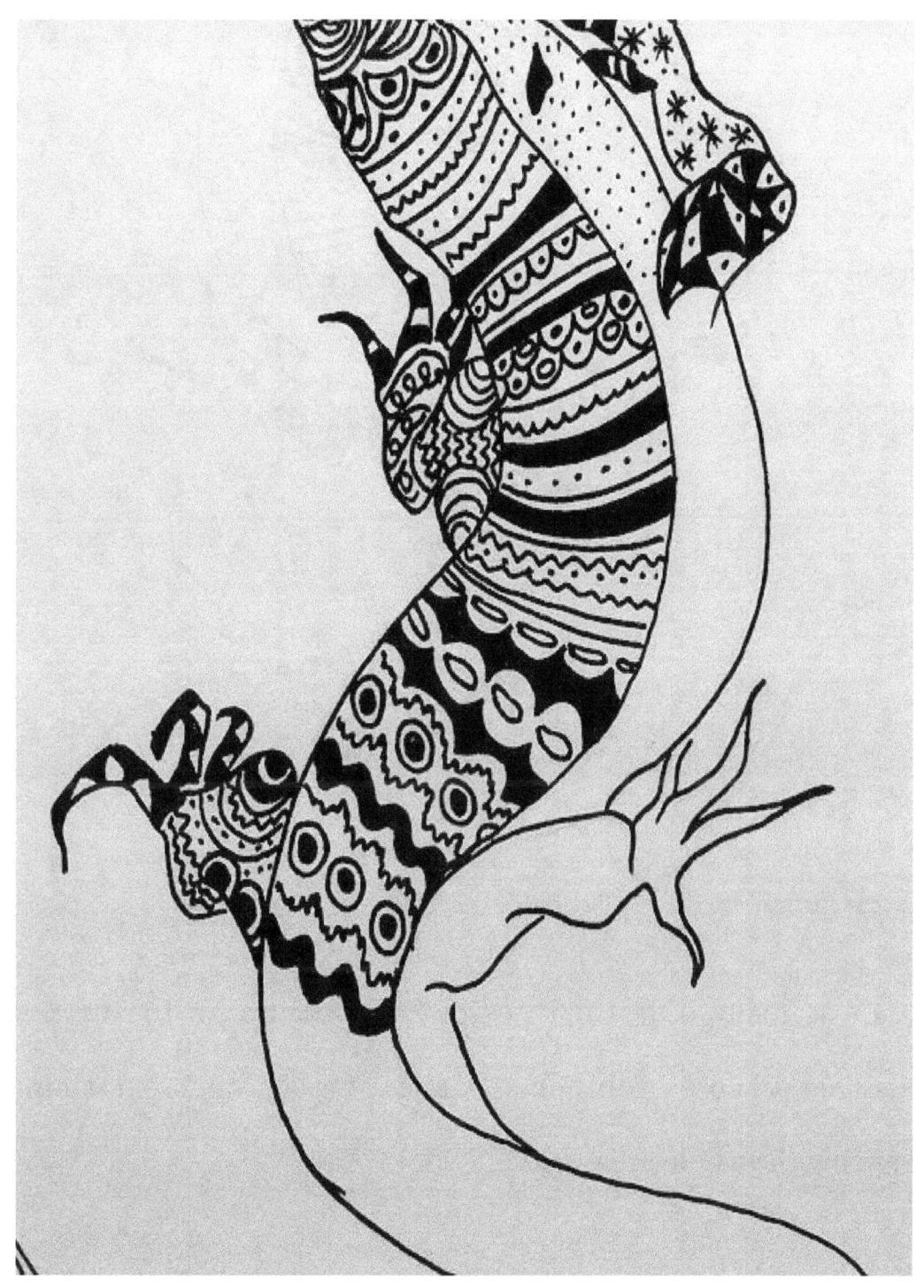

Move along the back line and to the tail.

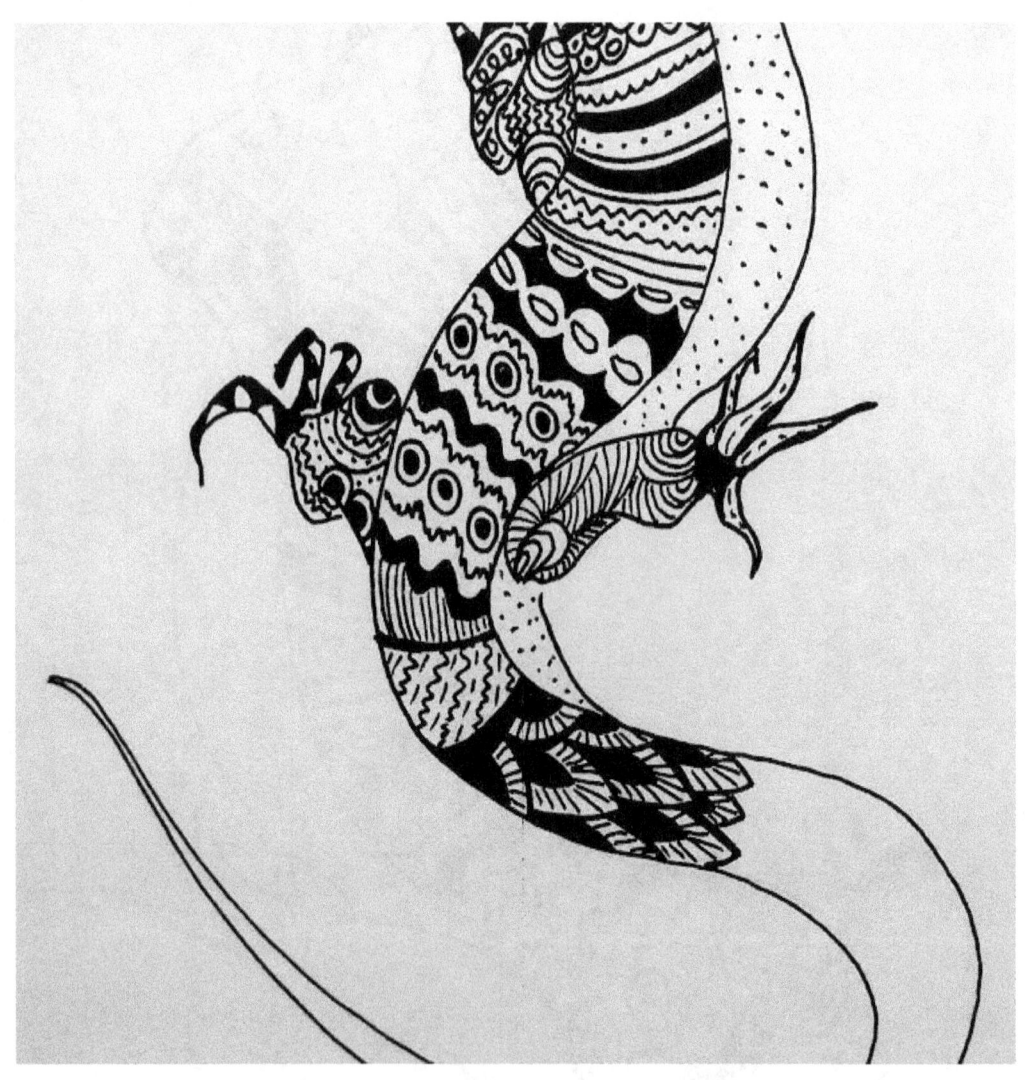

Draw as many different types of Zen Doodles on the back as possible. Choose from dots, circles, zigzag lines, to simply covering the whole area.

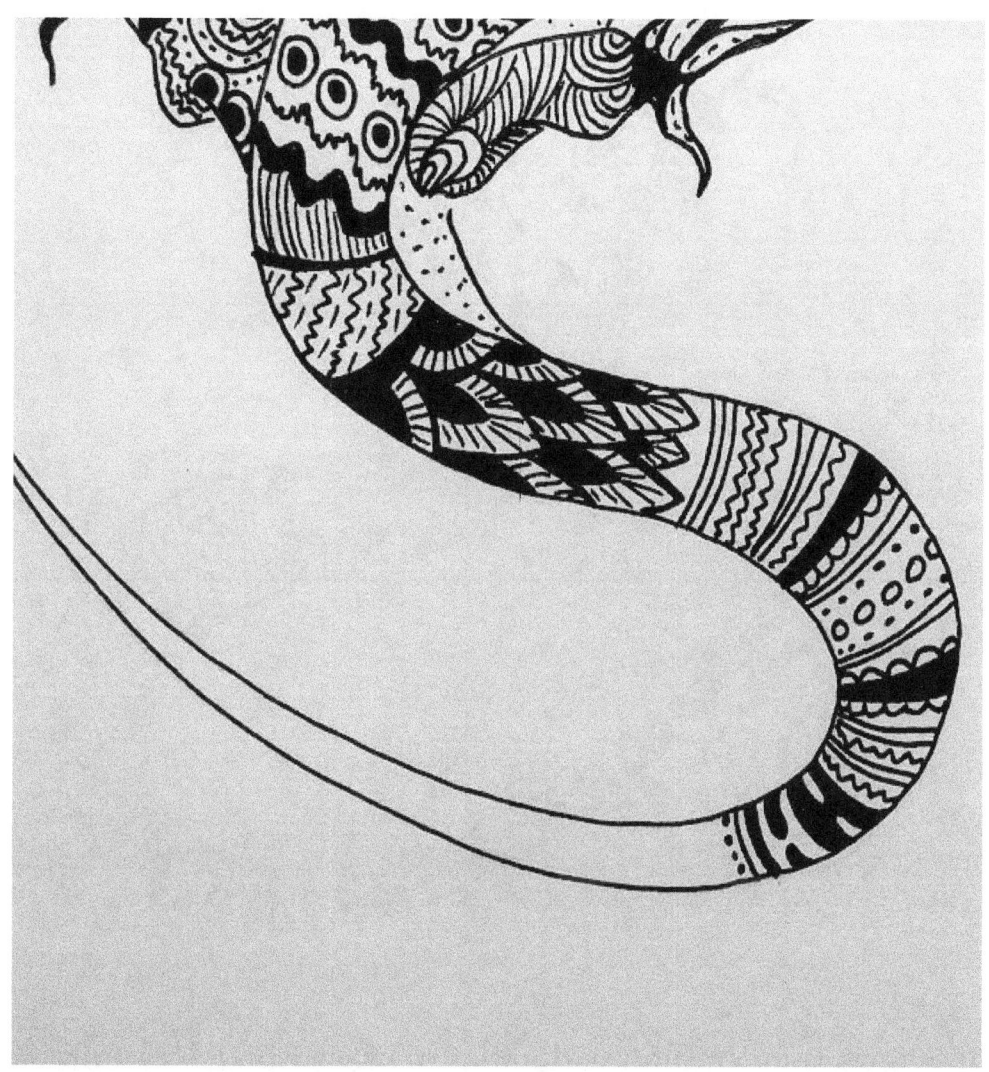

Finish the tail.

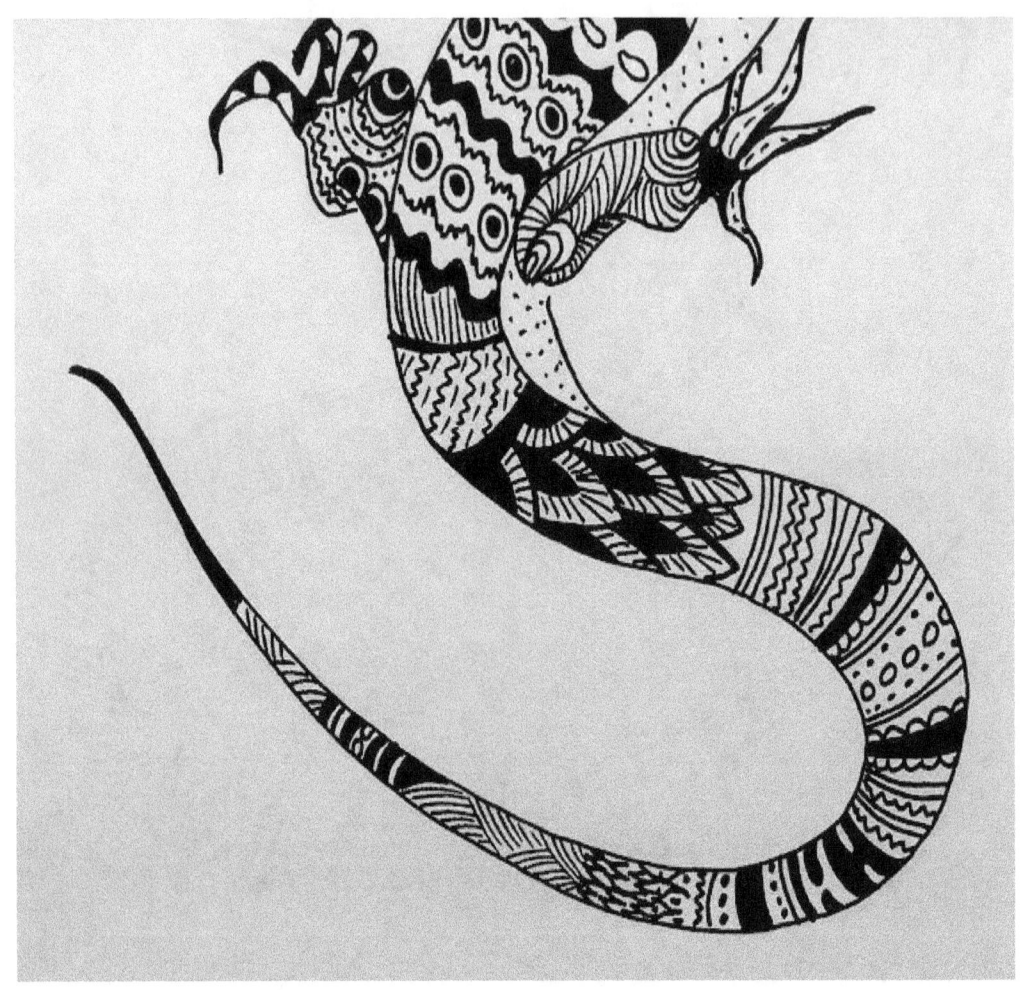

Make corrections by adding doodles in areas which look empty.

Your lizard drawing should be done by this point.

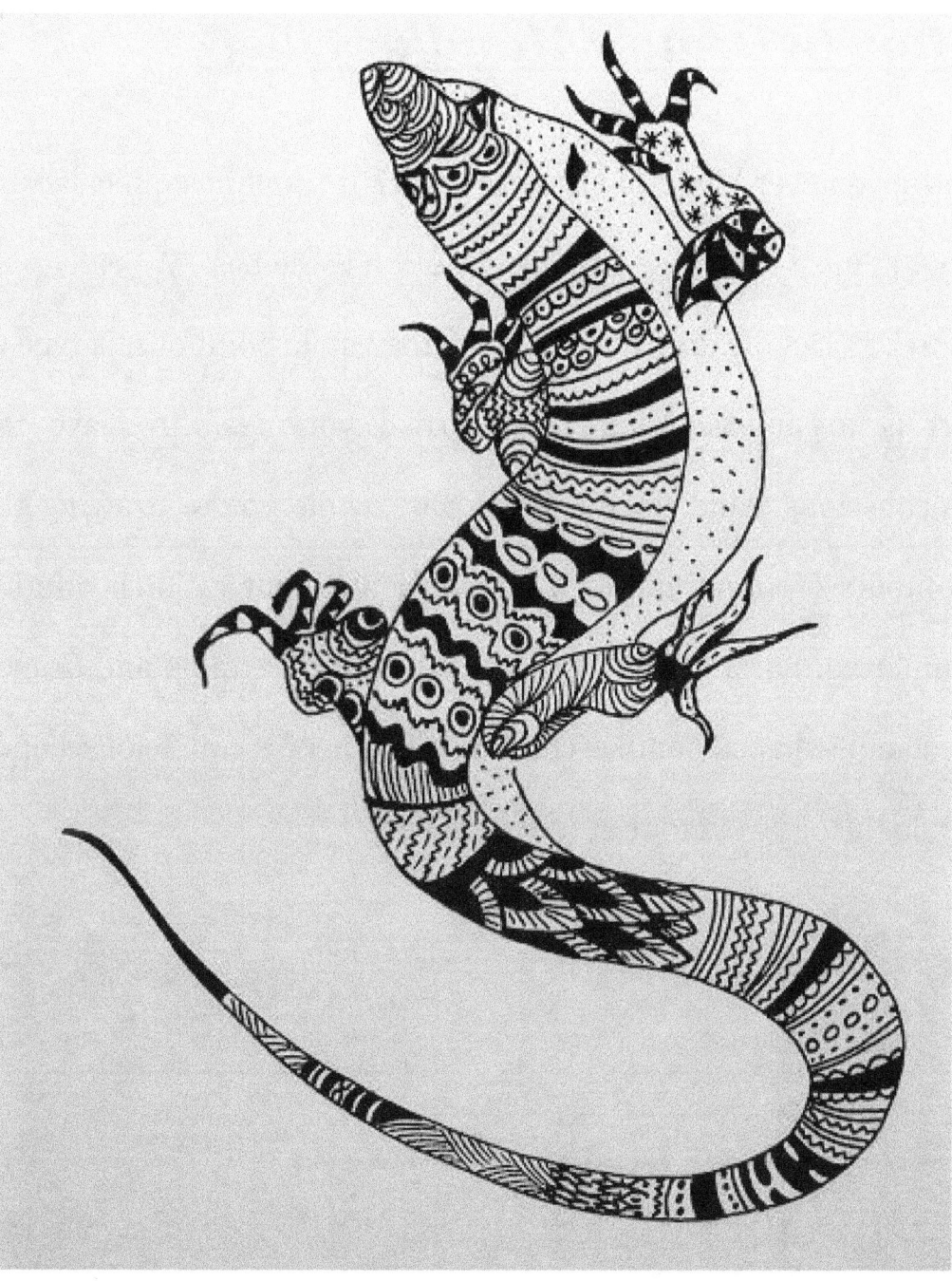

How to Draw a Handkerchief?

Have you ever heard of Occam's razor? It's a philosophical claim that in most cases, the simplest solution is the best. We can apply it to Zen Doodle drawing easily. As the whole point of this type of art is to unleash your inner artist, you need to leave the unconscious mind do the work. But, while you're drawing the contours of an animal or a human being, your rational mind is employed. So, it might be the best to keep it simple and draw a rectangle-shaped handkerchief. You just need a couple of seconds to do the basic contour at the beginning.

Add ornaments and draw curves.

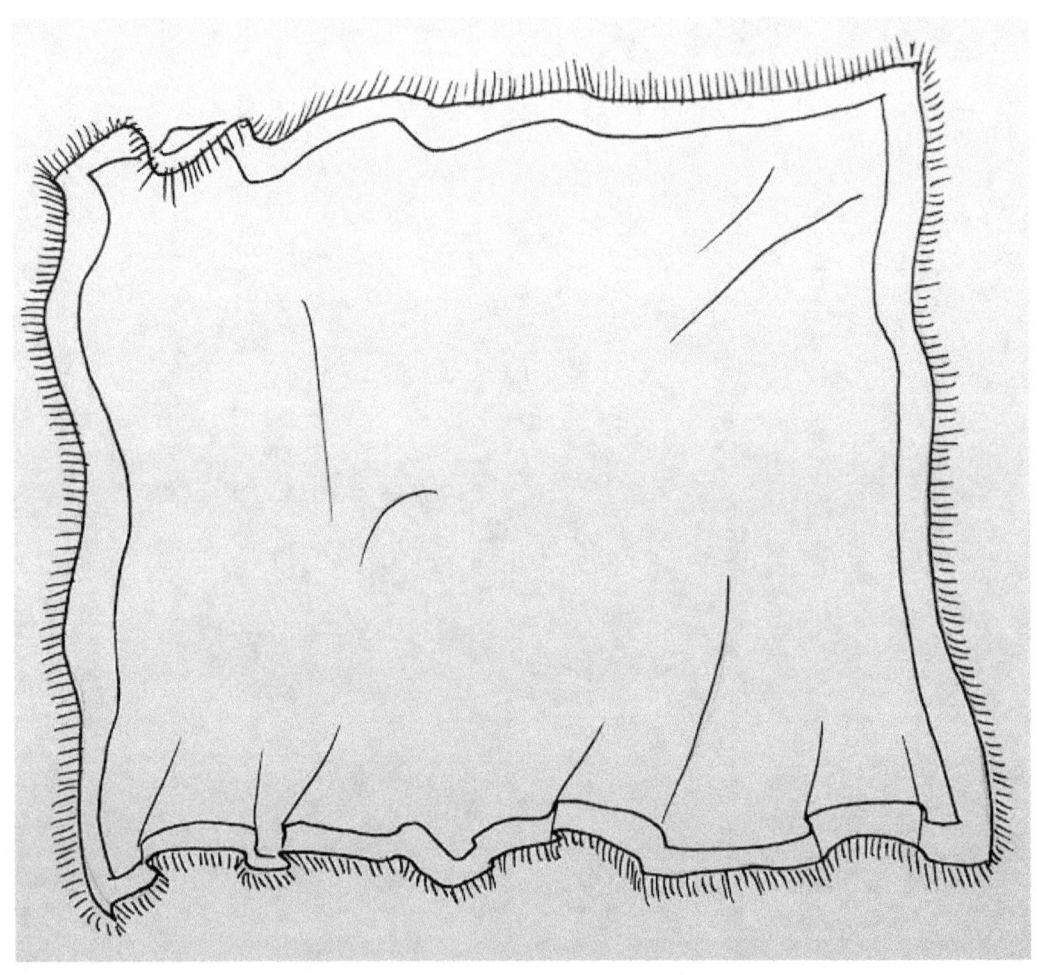

Start doodling from the near to the handkerchief border.

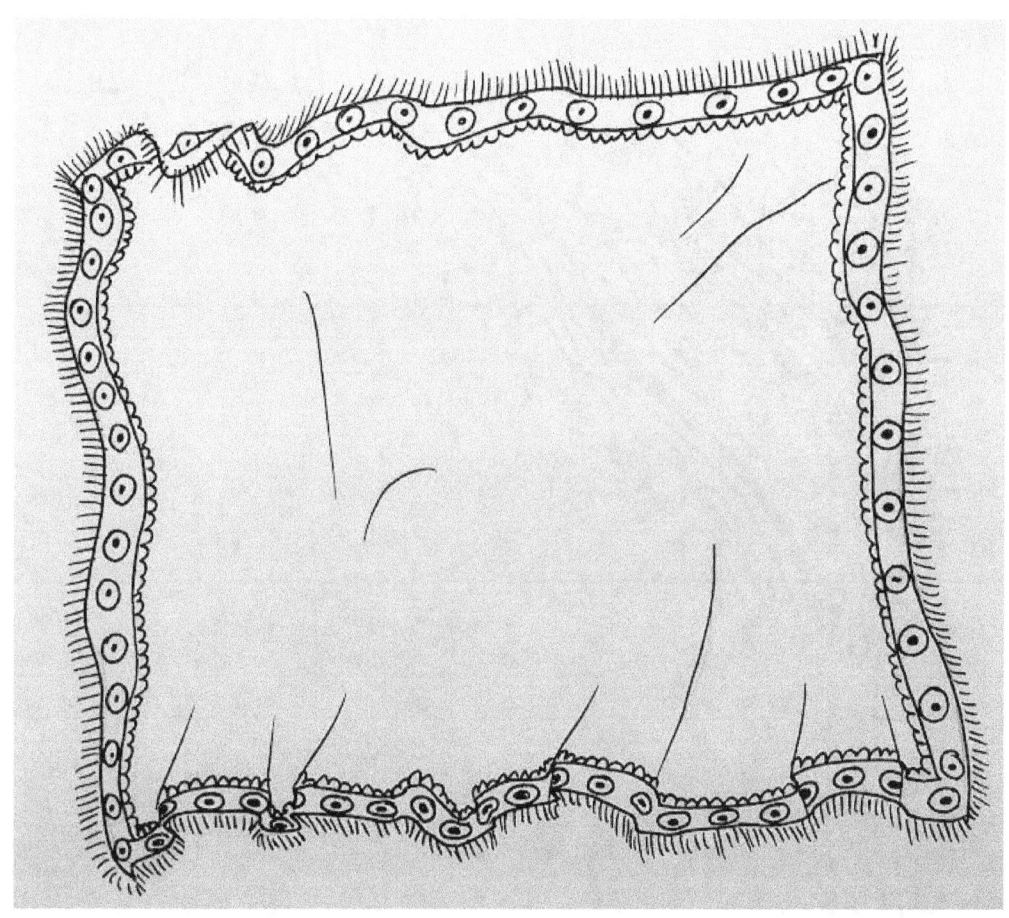

Once you're done with that, start filling the large area from the top left corner. Draw different types of lines, each connecting the left and the top side of the handkerchief.

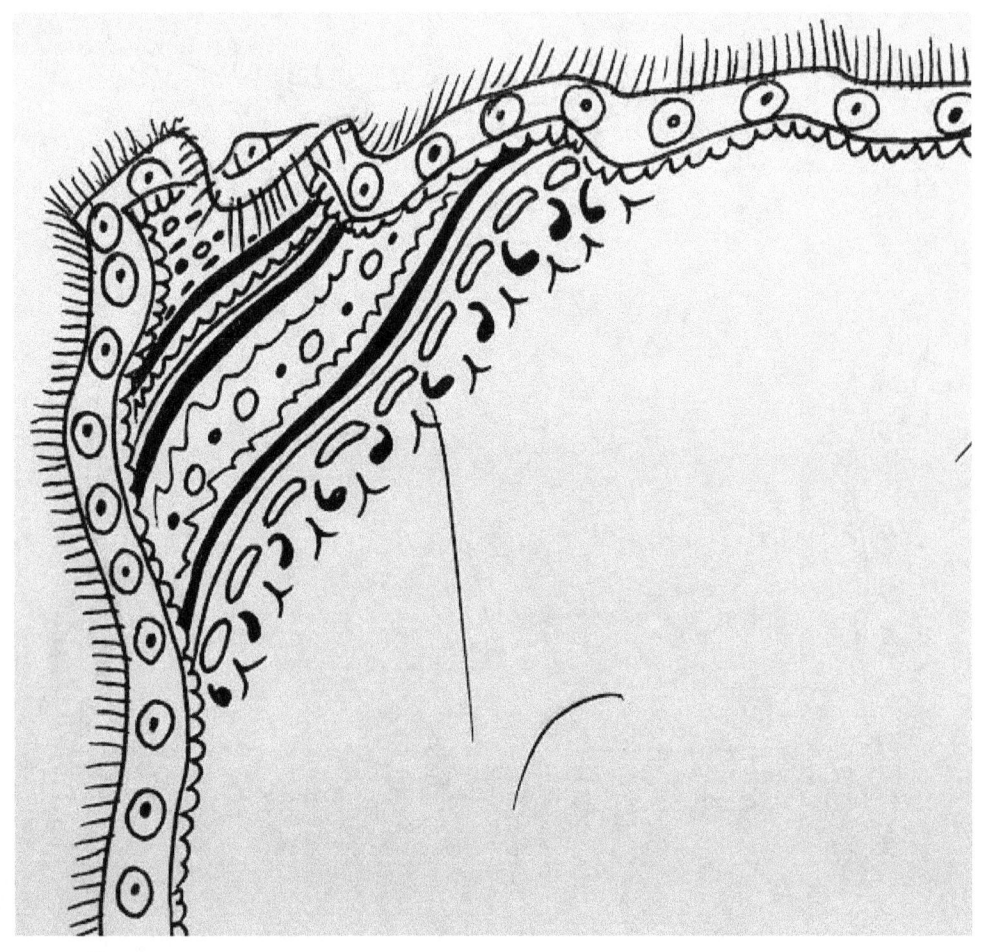

A couple of doodles there is enough before you move to another corner. Now, cover about one quarter of the whole area, starting from the bottom.

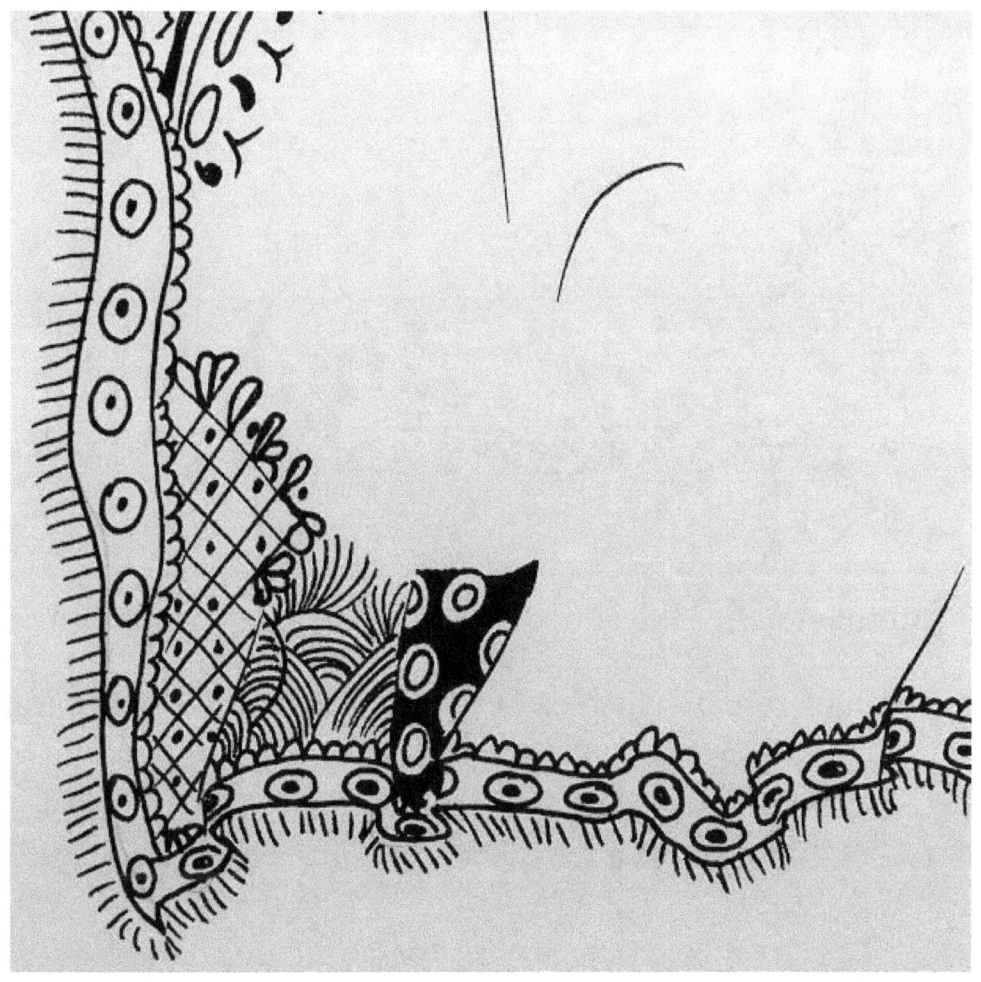

The example shows that you can draw bigger patterns on the

bottom.

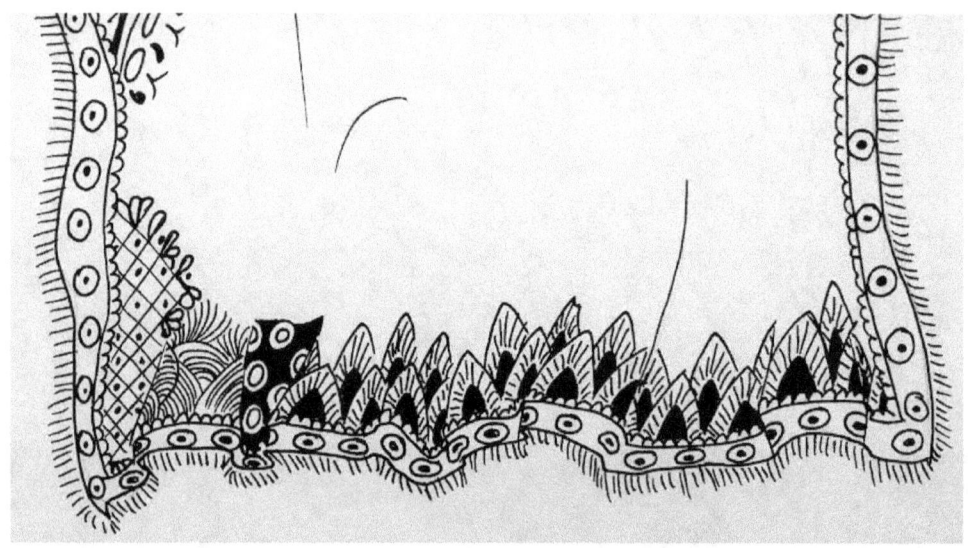

Be careful to fit the doodles so that the bends on the handkerchief remain visible. Let the bends be what separates doodle patterns.

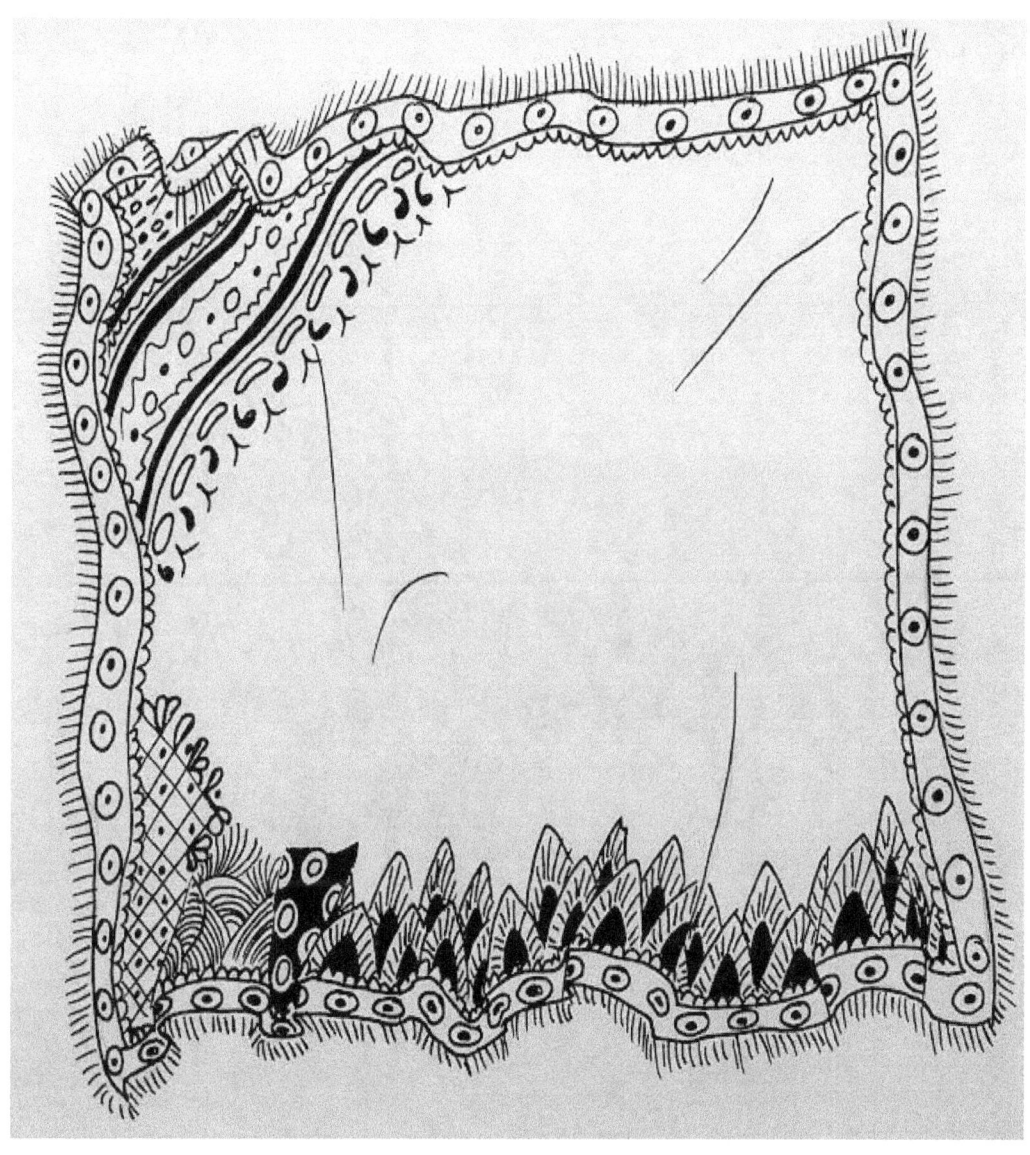

Do the right bottom corner.

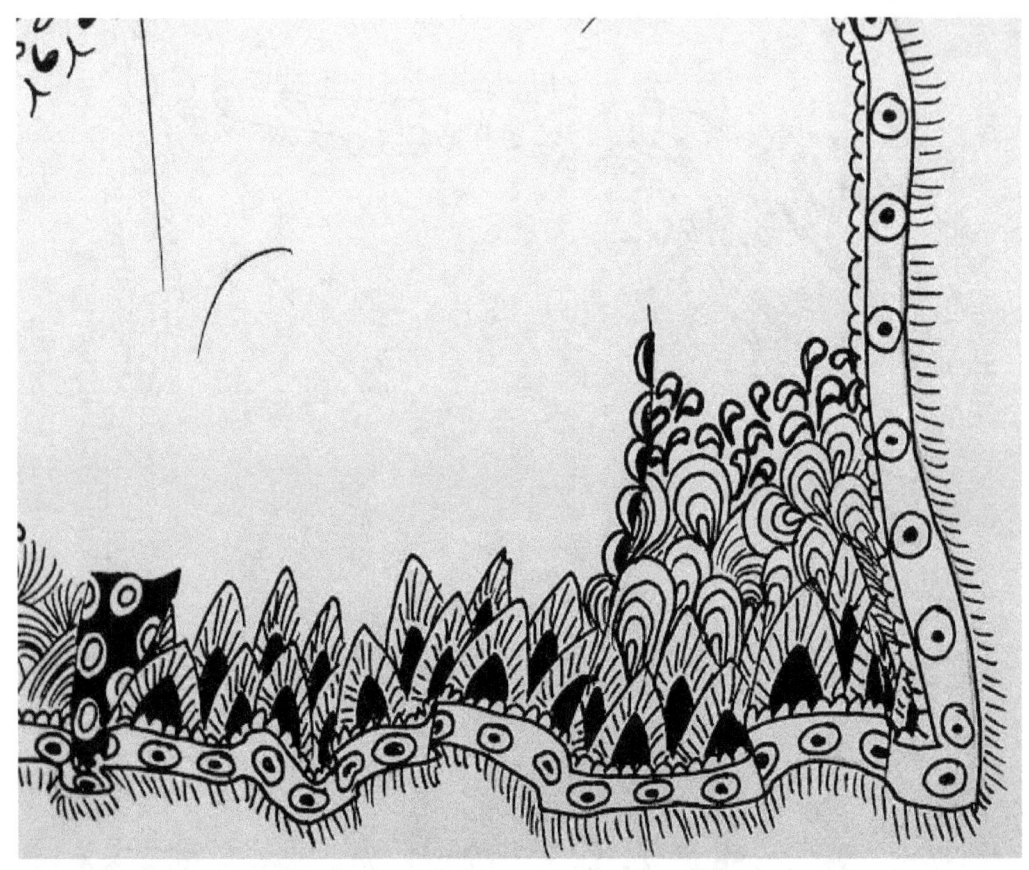

Join the bottom left with the top left corner with various doodles.

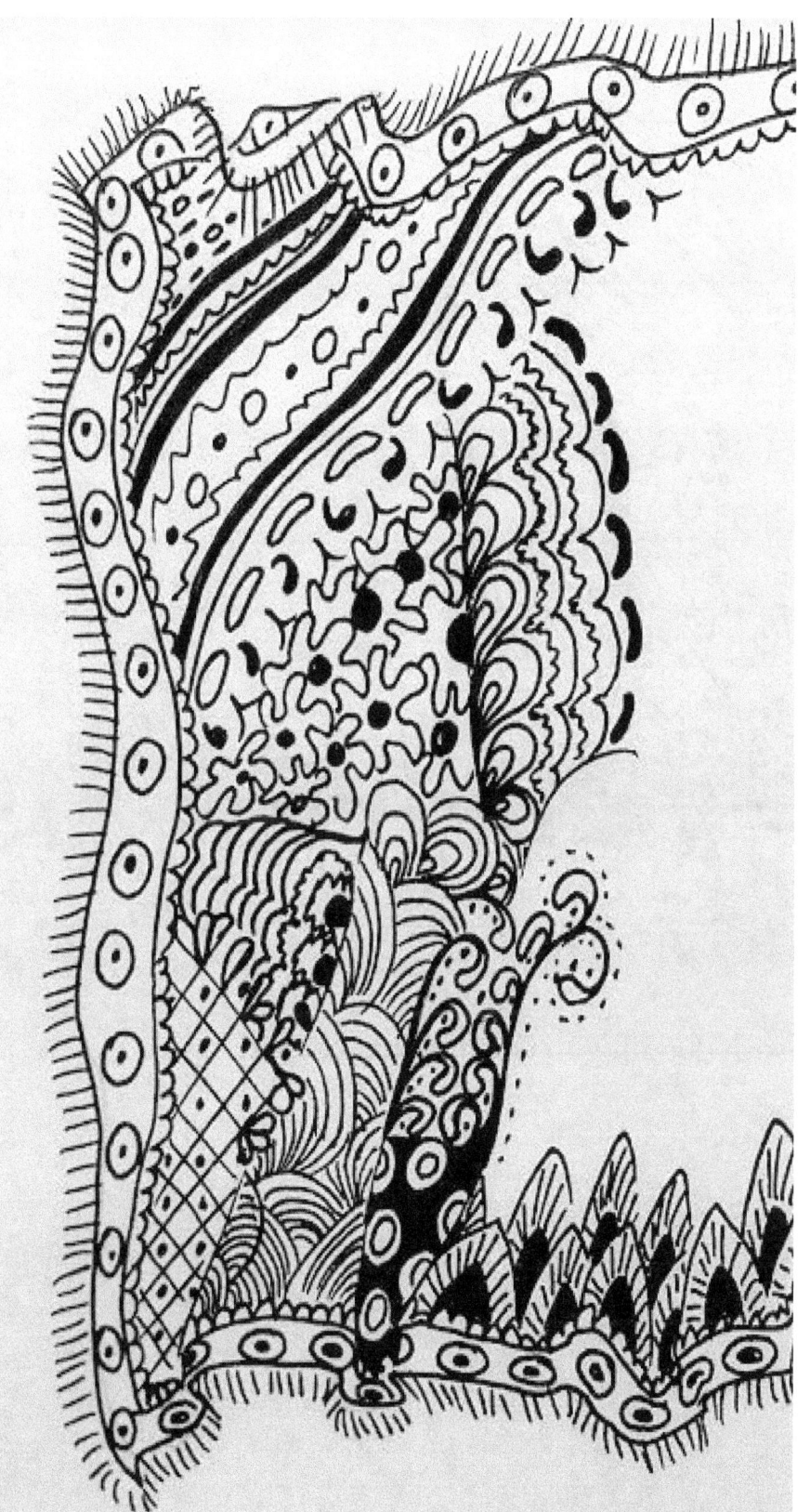

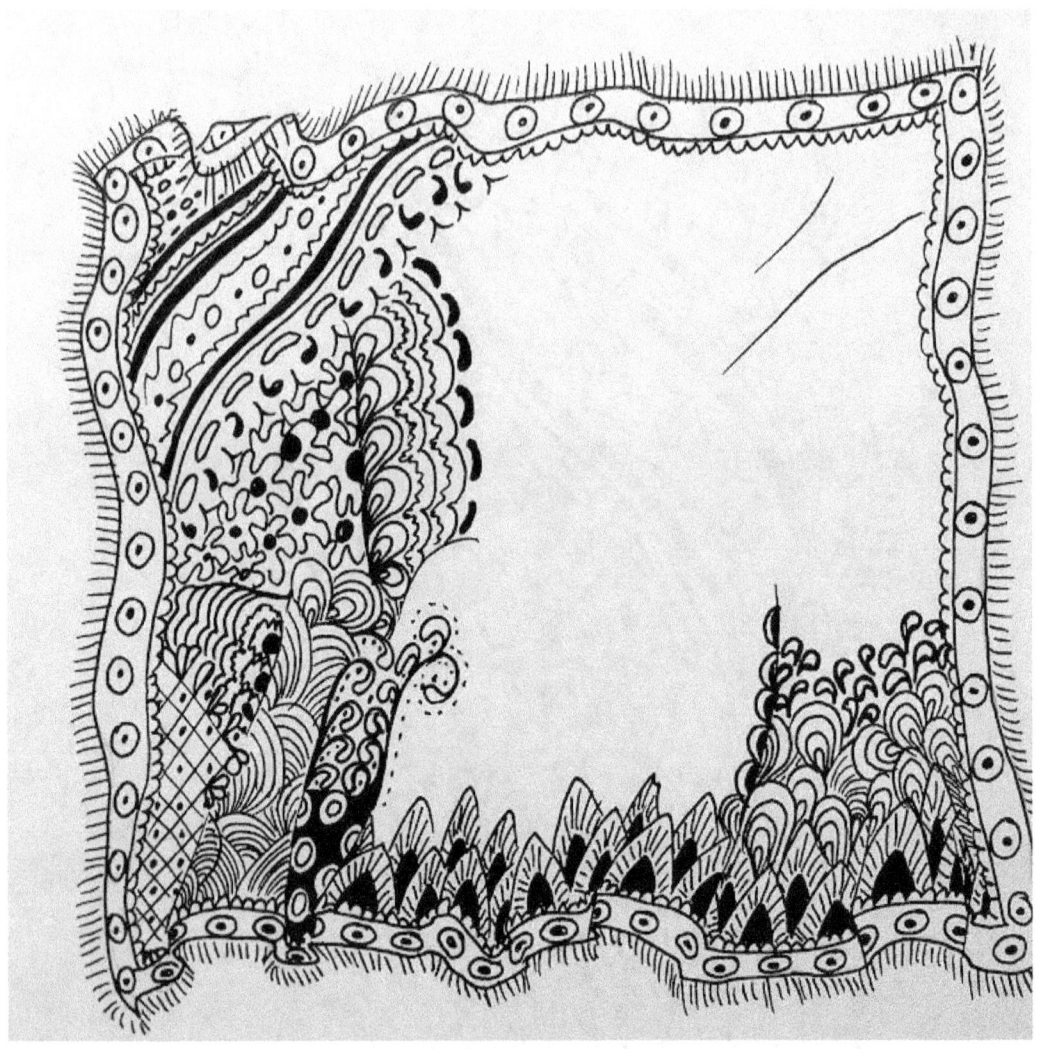

Move with doodling to the right top corner.

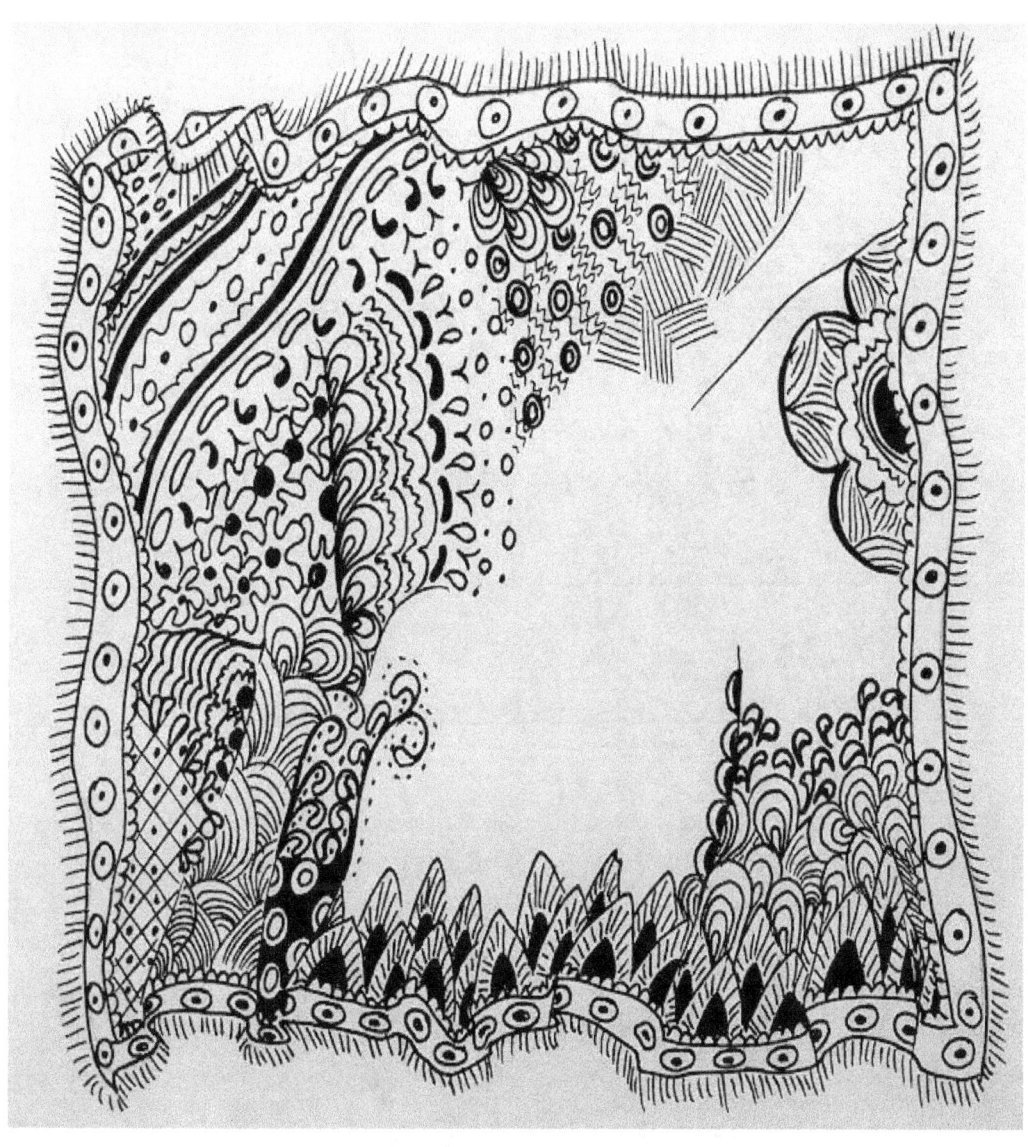

At this point, there's only the middle area that's blank.

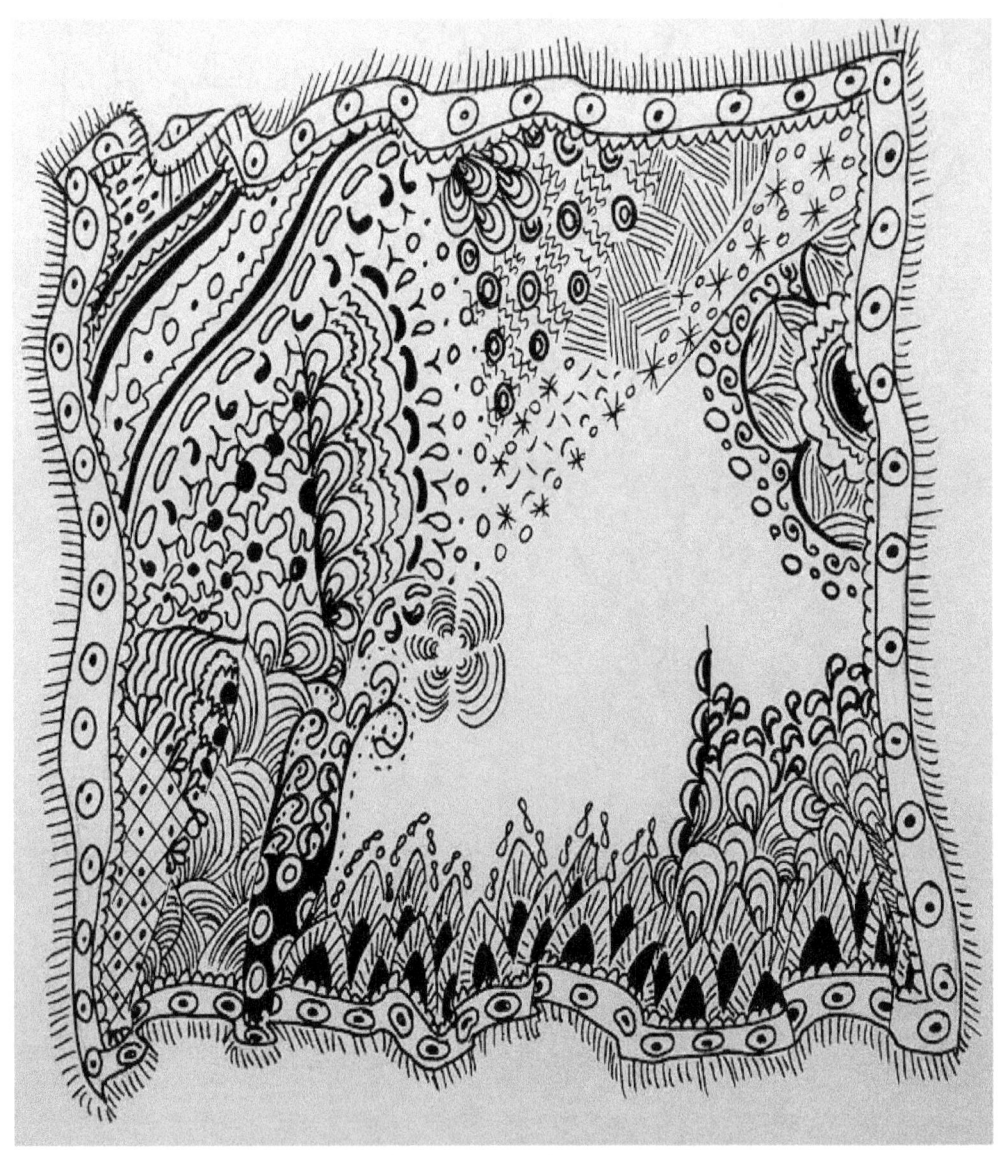

Fill everything that's left doodle-free.

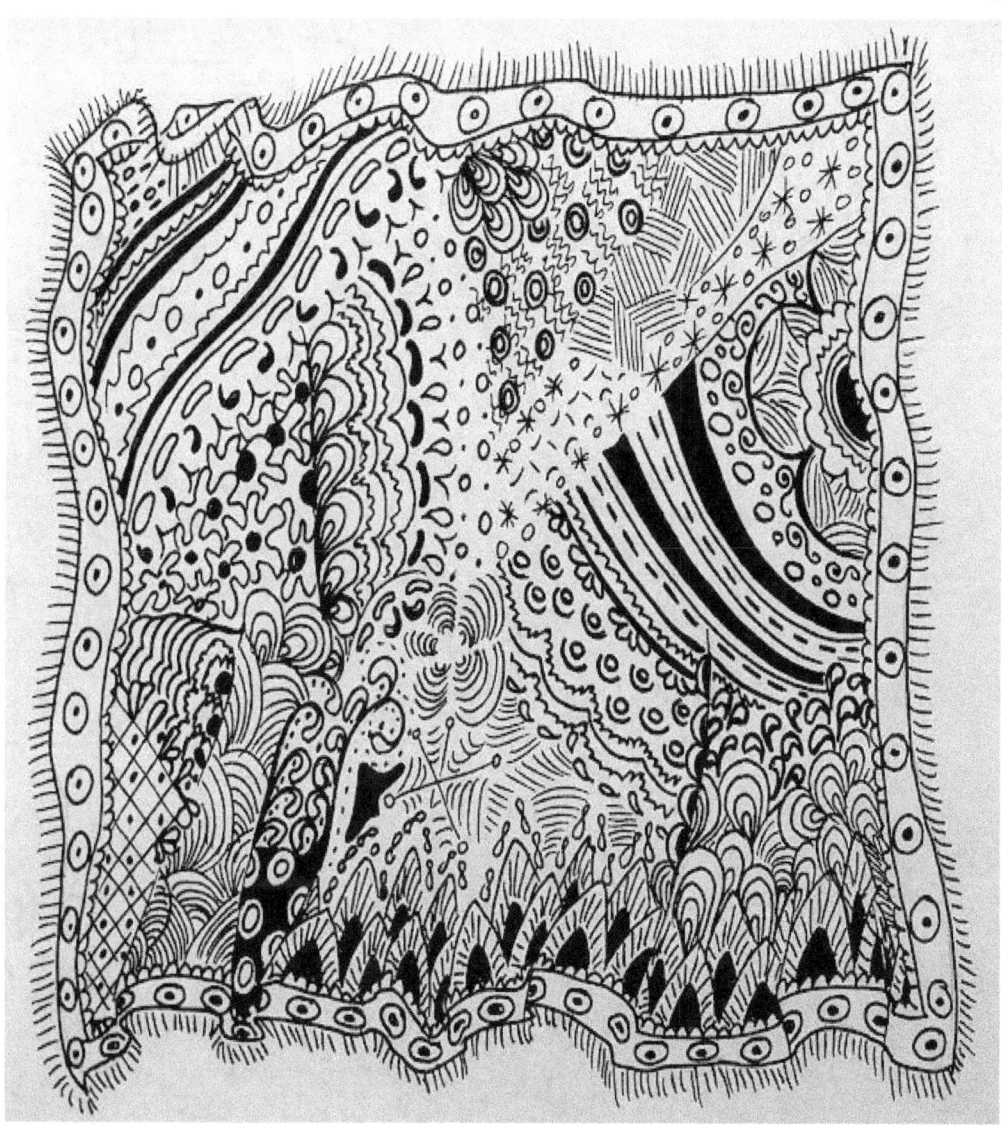

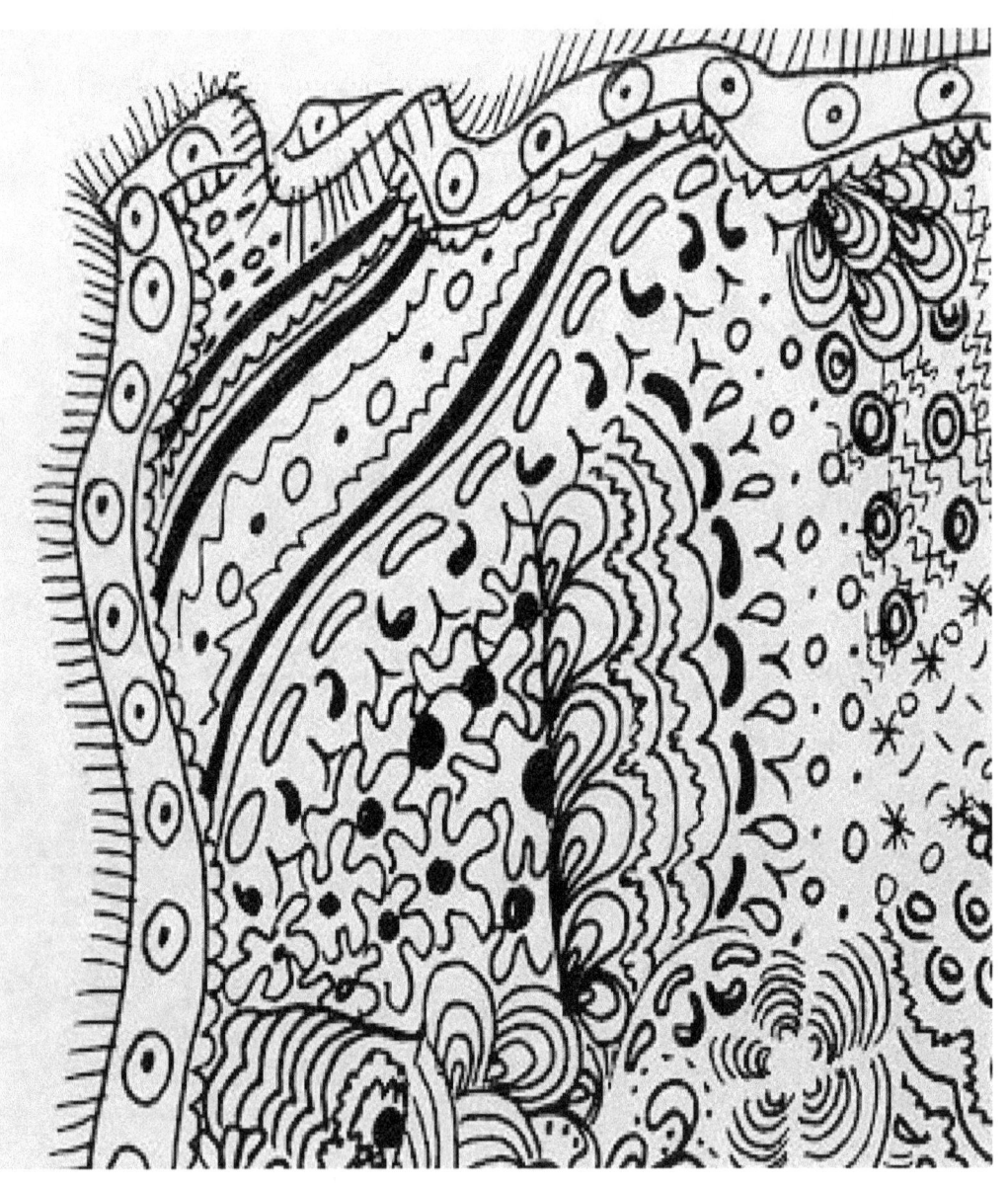

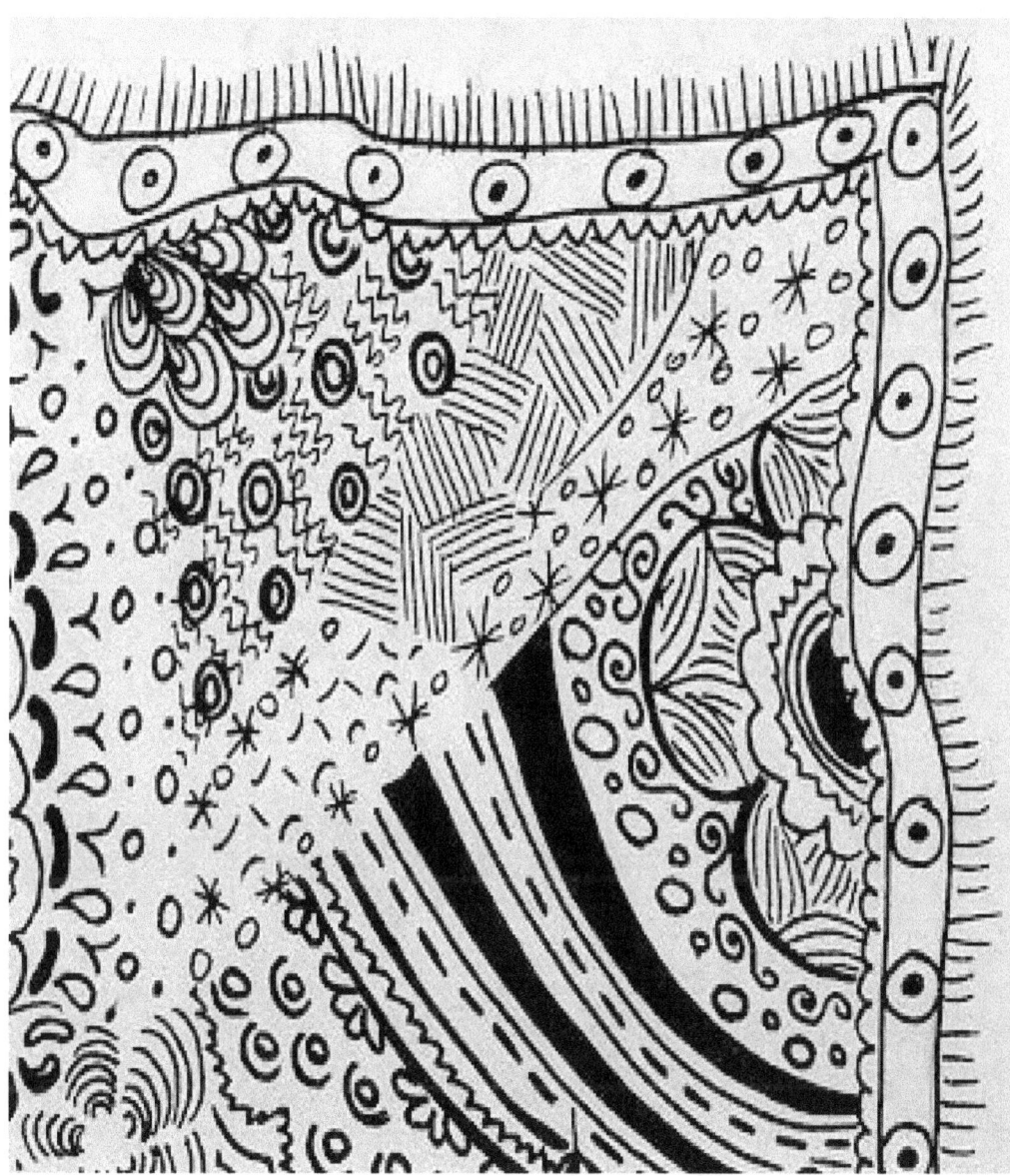

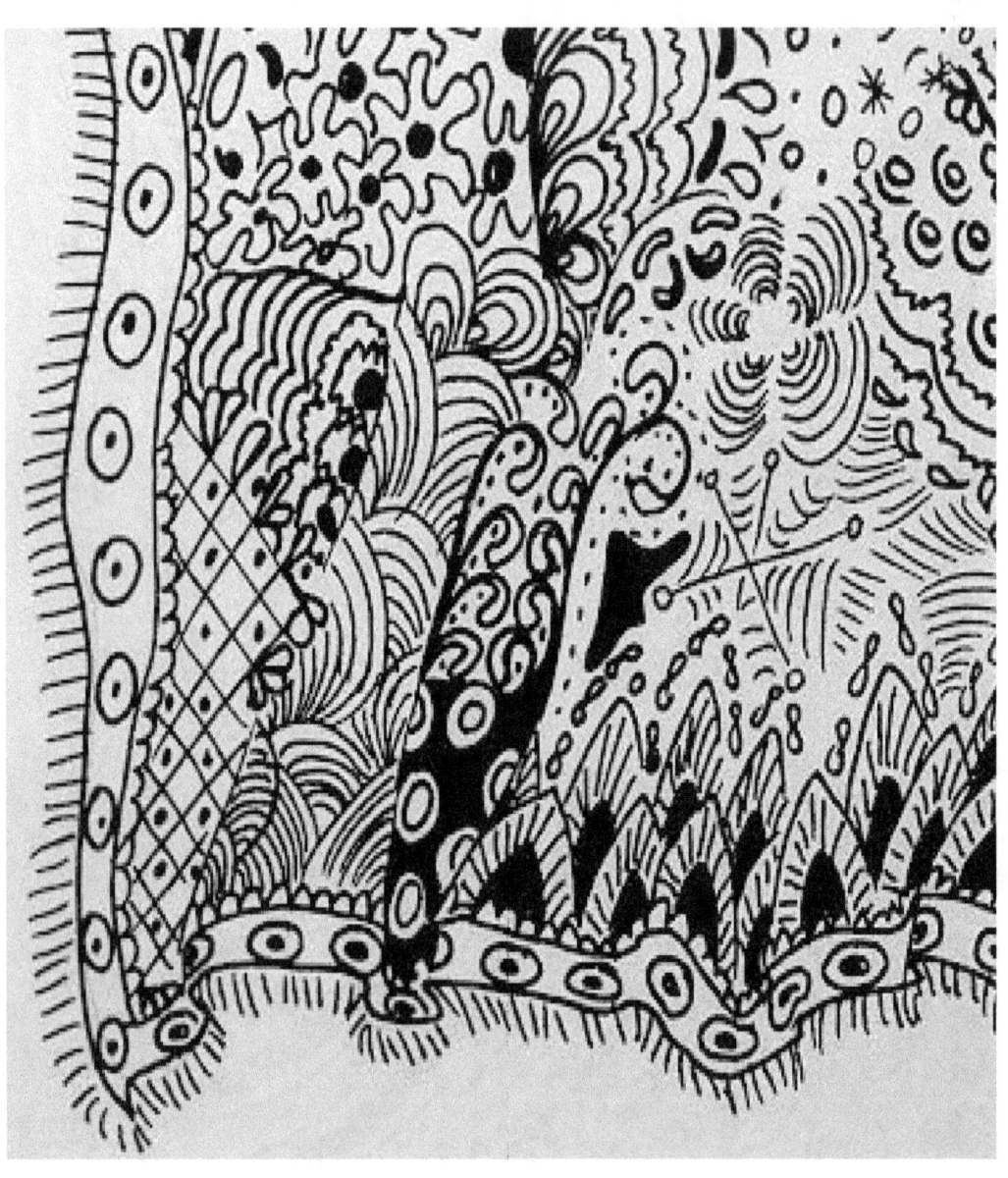

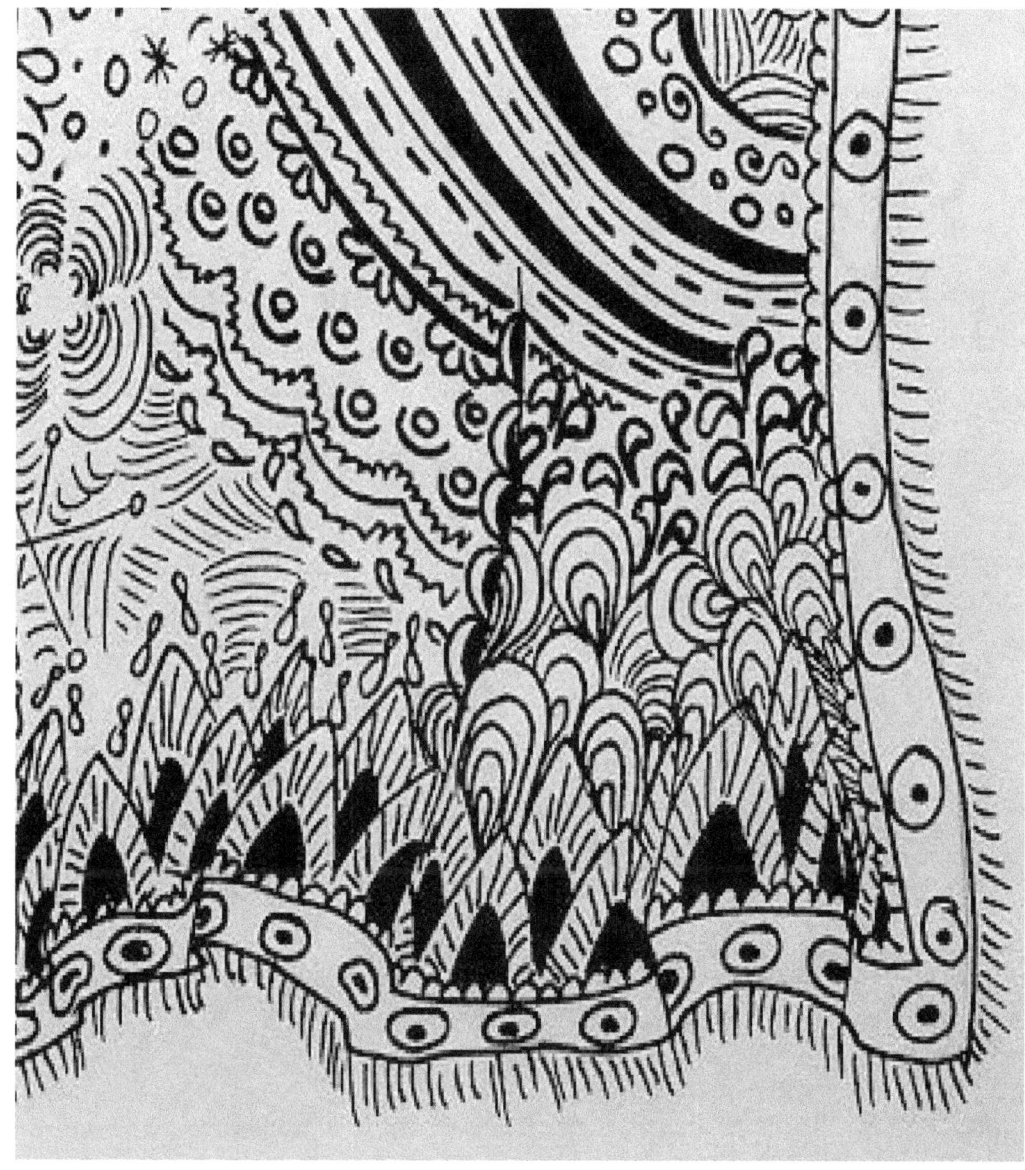

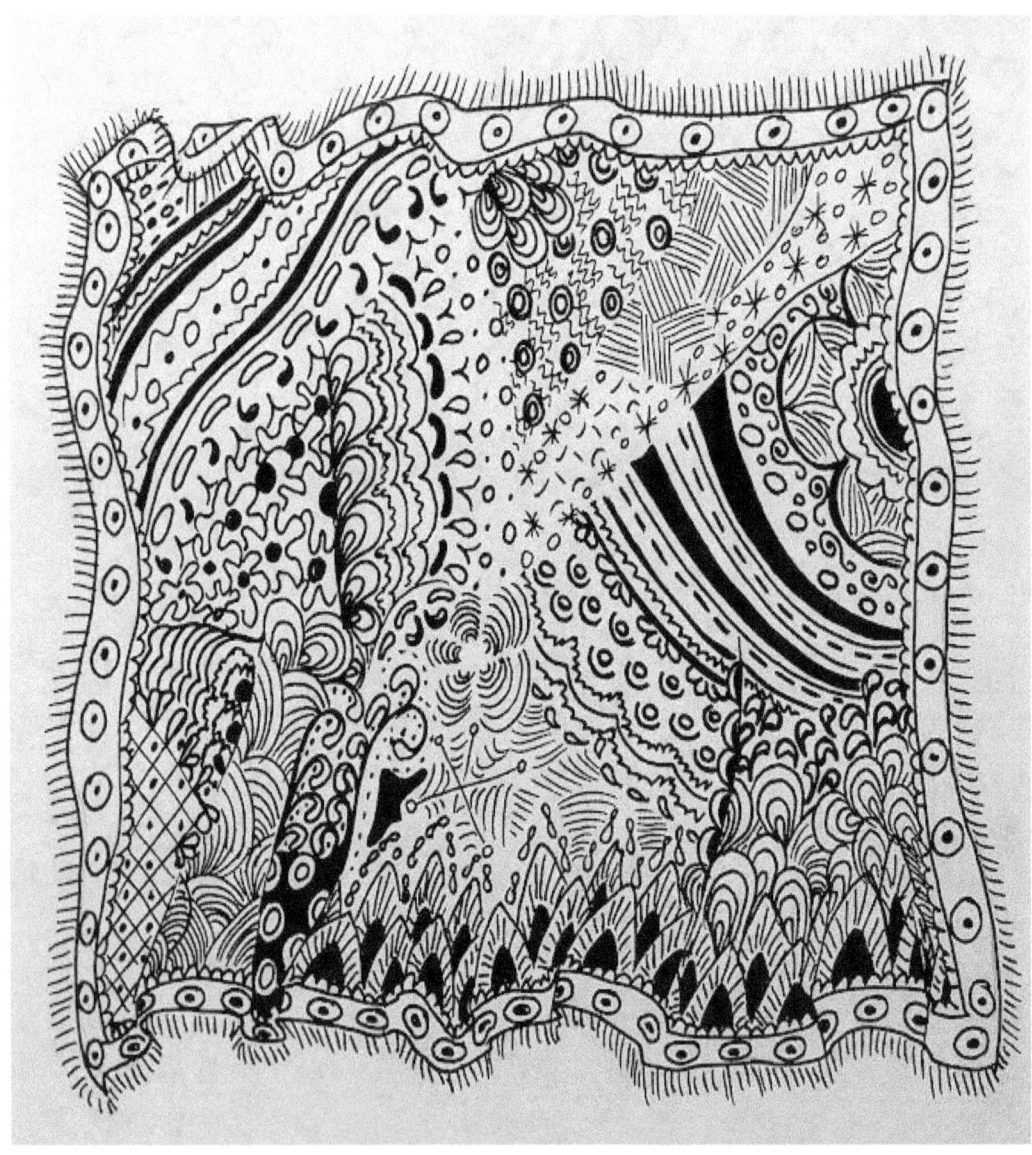

The final result should be something like this.

Chapter 3 – Zen Art Meditation

Zen Doodle drawing is a form of art meditation, allowing our minds to roam free and lead us throughout the practice of drawing. Zen Doodle drawing is a way of meditation that really works for a number of people, but some found it relaxing only to some extent. Still, one thing is certain – Zen Doodle drawing will broaden your horizons, thus making you more creative, even if you don't notice it at first glance.

Once you get into the so-called flow, the inspiration will rush and you'll be able to create beautiful drawings. But, that won't be limited only to drawing as this practice can influence your brain to be creative about an abundance of things. Some people have found that Zen Doodle drawing has turned their lives for the better.

It's an art form where you draw repetitive patterns. You have no end goal of the drawing, which allows your mind to be free from any obstacles and express its creativity to the fullest. There aren't many arts like Zen Doodle, which will help your mind produce exactly the art it wants.

Not only do Zen Doodle drawings look awesome, they can also have a lot of benefits for your mind and body. We've already mentioned that it opens up the mid and makes the one practicing it more creative, but there is much more to it. Many studies have been done in order to find out whether there's truth to these claims. Perhaps surprisingly, the research has shown that actually Zen Doodle drawing has more health benefits than anyone had expected.

Zen Doodle drawing is proven to have effect on mental and emotional health of the people, which is why it is recommended as a way of additional practice of all sorts of counseling. Zen

Doodle drawing also proved to be a great way to fight the battle with anxiety. Actually, a research has shown that cancer patients react nicely to it and report changes in their morale.

Just after a few weeks of practicing the Zen Doodle craft, some elderly patients have shown signs of progress in dealing with Alzheimer disease. The patients showed improvements in their motor skills almost instantly. Similar study was done with stroke patients and it produced the same results.

There are many anecdotes among Zen Doodle enthusiasts, many of which are claiming this art helped them sleep better and solve all kinds of other problems, including eating disorder. Of course, these claims are yet to be scientifically confirmed, but with so many people claiming it, there probably is some truth to it.

Chapter 4 – Subconscious Drawing

Zen Doodle drawing represents a conscious intention to turn the thoughts of a situation and intend to direct the attention to a particular shape that you draw. Therefore, this method belongs to consciously drawing types. Scribble like those to which we resort to when we are bored or when we make a phone call is directed drawing, and as such it can be called unconscious drawing. This shows a thing or two about the personality, so it is important that the forms emerge from depth of our consciousness when we are not focused.

Drawing as a form of therapy has positive effects on the mind and psyche of people, allowing them to establish a control over their focus and hand movements. Try it when you're angry and consciously direct your hand to draw a circle. You will notice that maybe your hand shakes or you grip a pen too hard, all of which are major indicators of how your body reacts. If you cannot calm down the mind, you can always calm down the hands and body. Zen Doodle drawing is one of the ways to calm yourself.

But don't draw solely when you're feeling stressed – do Zen Doodle drawings when you are calm, as well. Note the similarities and differences between the drawings that you draw when you were sad or angry and drawings when you are cam and happy. See which forms you used. Usually, when you're calm your Zen Doodle drawings will not have too many details on the circles, these are usually simple shapes with greater distances. When you're sad or angry, the drawings will have more details.

Psychologists suggest that all kinds of doodling can visualize your subconscious. Drawing Zen Doodles will bring you in touch with your mind, with what it really thinks. You can find out who you really are with this art. Zen Doodle drawing will help you unlock ideas that might have been stocked in your mind for ages.

If you think that you are bad at drawing, then you need a few lessons on how the subconscious mind works. You just need to let go and free your mind to do the rest. Passive drawing will squeeze all of the ideas stuck deep in the magic universe of the mind, making you amazed by the results. Once you visualize the subconscious, you will realize that you have an artist in you the whole time.

When you free yourself from all obstacles, your mind will become free. The mind will appreciate the freedom and will give a lot in return. But to free your mind is not an easy task. Even with Zen Doodle drawing, you still can be bothered by some everyday things. The only way to forget about them is to focus deeply on drawing. You'll realize that you are free once when you get yourself into the so-called flow. Flow is a strange thing, it can be described as a sudden boost of inspiration, but is actually much more than that.

You've probably felt the flow hundreds of times but didn't know how to explain the feeling. You know that when you're doing something, whether is your job or a hobby, at one point you'll get to a state of mind when you are so focused that you do not notice that the time is passing. The moment when you forget about everything except the work you're doing is the start of a flow.

To get in the state of a flow, you need to find the thing you're doing funny and motivational. That's why Zen Doodling is great – it allows you to draw anything you want, without any boundaries. If you feel like drawing a circle, do so. If you want to draw a continuous line, nothing's stopping. Let the imagination go wild!

You will notice that your Zen Doodle drawings change constantly. One day you'll be drawing circles, the other you're preferred shape will be triangle. It might seem pointless to keep the artwork, but that's far from the truth. The Zen Doodle drawings are a real proof of your state of mind at this period of life. You can always use them in future to get a reflection on a certain period of life. For example, you can see what kind of drawings you made when you were working for a certain company. If they appear like a stressed person had drawn them, then you should not think about getting better to that firm. Saving your artwork can also be very helpful in your love life, finding about how you felt about a certain person.

Chapter 5 – Zen Doodle Coloring Books for Adults

Creative coloring books for adults that have emerged on the market are made on the principle of Zen Doodle drawings. So, basically you have a collection of different Zen Doodle drawing works that you can paint as you like. The appearance of these coloring books is important for several reasons:

- It reminds adults that do not need to grow up. Painting and drawing are skills that need to cultivate for therapeutic reasons, as these skills are a part of mental hygiene.

- It deepens the relationship between parents and children. This coloring book is definitely a good way of spending quality time.

-Because of all of the reasons mentioned, adults can gain insight into what they draw, they can become calmer and more focused.

- It boosts creativity. Same as any type of craft, coloring Zen Doodle paintings is a great way to become more creative and produce new ideas.

Analyzing your drawings can infer a lot about yourself, but can be a lot of fun at the same time. On top of that, coloring Zen Doodle drawings could mean that you'll creates something really awesome, which you'll be able to use for other things like decorating your home, clothes, etc.

We agree that adult coloring books can be a great deal of fun, but it can't compare with the pleasure of doing your own Zen Doodle draw. If you start from scratch with the drawing, you will put a lot of your personality in it. This claim might seem strange, but when you're doing a Zen Doodle drawing, you're literary putting your emotions down on the paper. Because of that, if you do it all the way from the beginning, you will be much more proud of the final work. And of course, your personal Zen Doodle drawing can serve as an adult coloring book. The only difference it has with the ones you can get in shops is that your Zen Doodle drawing

book is completely free!

Chapter 6 – Crafts Similar to Zen Doodling

Mandala drawing is a similar craft to Zen Doodle drawing, thus having similar effects on the mind. The word mandala means circle in Sanskrit, is called also a magic circle. As a symbol it's not only linked to the East; in many other cultures mandala is presented in the form of flowers. In the classic sense, mandala is a projection of the world, the cosmic intelligence, as well as the unity of macro and microcosms. Mandala is also an instrument for visualization and meditation. You can find on the Internet plenty of mandalas that can help you in meditating.

Carl Gustav Jung was a pioneer in the study of the structure of the mandala. Almost 25 years he studied the mandala and noticed that the person who draws them subconsciously draws circles on paper. It was later discovered through a research that mandalas can be an important instrument in the view of one's mental condition. Much has been dealt with the unconscious while displaying the symbols as forms of expression. He studied the cultural and civilization aspect of mandalas, but devoted most attention to the psychological aspect.

Drawing mandalas is not difficult. There are no special skills you need for drawing them. You just need a pair of compasses, ruler, paper and paint. You can use felt-tip pens, or you can use wax, watercolor, acrylic, again, depends on the surface on which you draw the mandala. The point is that the line from the center of the mandala in the form of concentric circles that spread outwards. The distance between these circles may or may not be the same. It is important to know that you if draw in one part of the circle you should do the same in all parts - it is essential symmetry. If you do not have a divider, you can draw a circle by hand or use a circular contour of an object.

Differences between drawing mandalas and Zen Doodle drawings:

1. Mandala has the form of a circle or the square. Zen Doodle drawing shapes do not necessarily have to be in the form of a circle or square.

2. Mandala patterns are repeated in all parts of the circle. The principle of symmetry is not required for Zen Doodle drawing.

3. Mandalas should be painted, Zen Doodle drawings are usually done in black and white version, although nothing is stopping you from painting them.

4. In drawing mandalas, you can use the eraser, while Zen Doodle drawing does not allow the use of it.

Conclusion

Psychologists like Sigmund Freud and Carl Gustav Jung have claimed that without a free mind, there is no creativity. The modern scientists agree with these two psychology giants and add that thinking "outside of the box" can benefits all areas of life, not only art. But lateral thinking is not easy – you don't have the "Eureka moments" every second. That is why you need to work on your creative mind and one of the best ways to do that is with a creative art, such as Zen Doodle drawing.

There is no doubt that Zen Doodle drawing will open up your brain, but that is not all it will do. We have dedicated a whole chapter to Zen art meditation. Zen Doodle drawing puts your mind in a different state, the so-called flow. During the flow, the time goes by and you're not noticing it. You get relaxed and focused only on one thing – the drawing. This is exactly the same thing the traditional meditation does, so are allowed to call the Zen Doodle drawing a type of meditational activity.

There are reports that Zen Doodle drawing produces a list of benefits to the human body and brain, some of which include the prevention of Alzheimer's disease, fighting anxiety and depression, as well as helping a good night sleep.

Finally, even if you're not suffering from the problems mentioned above, nor you need to free your mind, you can still do Zen Doodle drawing just for fun. Let's face it, this is one of the most interesting crafts. On top of that, it's fairly easy, allowing everyone to create art works for almost free.

Thank you!

We hope you enjoyed the Zen Doodle trip with Elizabeth Stone and now you can Doodle whatever you like with various patterns.

We are happy to recommend you the other book by Elizabeth Stone:

ZEN Doodle Art: New Zen Doodle Patterns - Step by Step Guide

https://www.amazon.com/dp/B01C4G7UJ6

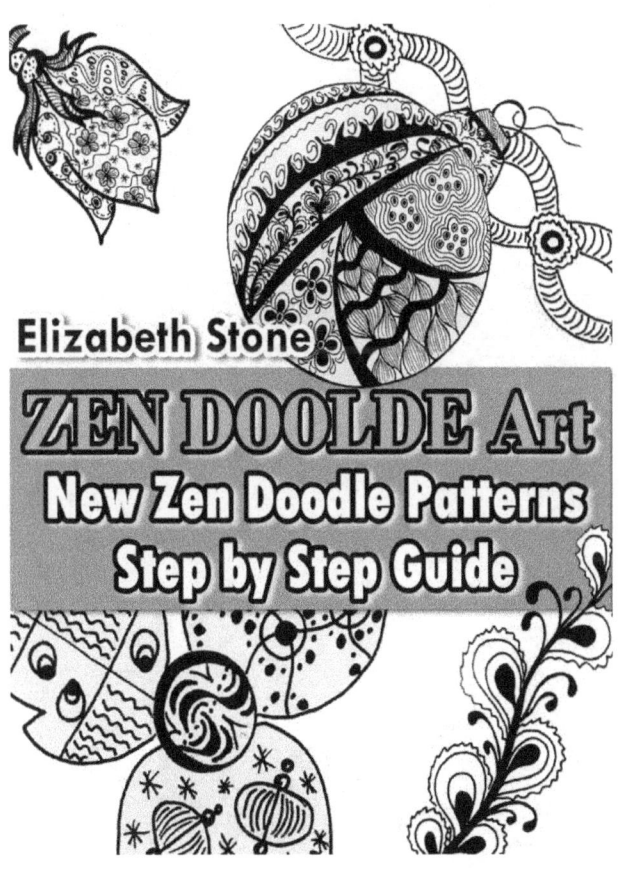

www.ingramcontent.com/pod-product-compliance
Lightning Source LLC
Chambersburg PA
CBHW080712190526
45169CB00006B/2348